The Presidential Trend

*The Remarkable Voting Predictability
of the Office of President*

Tony Fairfax

The Presidential Trend
The Remarkable Voting Predictability of the Office of President

Book Code: TPT1XA26YZ

Cover Photo by: Kaufmann Visual Arts

International Standard Book Number: 9-78-097525467-7

Library of Congress Control Number: 2012955251

First Edition Printing: December 2013

CONTENTS

The Presidential Trend

LIST OF FIGURES

v

The Presidential Trend

LIST OF TABLES

DEDICATION

To my extraordinary parents, Nathaniel & Helen Fairfax

Tony

The Presidential Trend

ACKNOWLEDGMENTS

Rarely do I get an opportunity to thank those who have helped me along the long road that ultimately led to the development of this book. Therefore, I thought that I would take this opportunity to thank a partial list of the people who have assisted me to the place I am today. First, special love and thanks to my wife, Colita, and my daughters, Layla and Natalie, for their enormous love and support during the creation of this book. Tremendous appreciation goes to my brother, Rick Fairfax, for being the model of a steadfast religious devotee throughout most of my life. Great gratitude from me to my extended family of the Nichols and McKissicks.

I would also like to say thanks to my small group of first cousins—Leslie, Stephanie, Steve, Reah, Eric—and to my wonderful aunts and uncles, some of whom have passed. Thanks for those little enjoyable moments growing up; to my cousin Monique and our friend Janet, thanks for introducing me to some neat media folk; to my oldest buddy J, whom I have known for almost a lifetime, thanks for all of the business projects; to the fellows who got me through college at VA Tech: Burn, D, Irv, Joe, J Smith, and O. I probably would not have a degree without you guys (or was it that I almost did not get a degree because of you guys); to the wonderful folks at Teledyne Hastings Raydist and EER Systems, working at those companies gave me a sound basis for my career; to Sharon and Bill, we gave it a try at ETC; to Winnett at DS and Rudy at NSU, thanks for some very interesting and challenging work that literally changed my life; to Anita (one of the best voting rights attorneys in the country) and Allison at the SCSJ, you two's professionalism and social justice dedication inspired me to work harder; and to many great individuals in the city of Hampton, VA, thanks for making it a great place to live.

Finally, I would like to thank those who were part of the organization that I was working for when I discovered the trend, the CBC Institute. Thanks Janice, Marsha, Andrea, Art, and the rest of the board. To the original board members of congress: Clyburn, Hilliard, Kilpatrick, C. Meek, Thompson, and, last but not least, Watt, thanks for increasing my faith in our legislative system. Regina and my namesake Tony H, you two made the second tour at the CBCI very enjoyable.

All of these individuals in some small or large way contributed to my growth as a person and thus ultimately to this book. I thank you all.

SPECIAL ACKNOWLEDGEMENTS

I would like to state a special thanks to all of the Kickstarter supporters that ensured that this book would be published.

The Presidential Trend

ABOUT THE AUTHOR

Currently, Mr. Fairfax is president and CEO of CensusChannel LLC, a demographic and mapping consulting company. However, he began his career working as an electrical/hardware design engineer for a manufacturing division of Teledyne Inc. and then for an engineering consulting firm, Engineering and Economic Research Systems.

Nevertheless, for over 20 years, Mr. Fairfax has worked providing mapping and demographic consulting services. Specializing in redistricting, he has developed several hundred plans that covered 22 different states. His plan analysis and development support covers the 1990, 2000, and more recently, 2010 round of redistricting.

During the span of his consulting tenure, Mr. Fairfax has provided redistricting services and training to numerous major nonprofit and public sector groups. A partial list of these organizations include: Advancement Project; Congressional Black Caucus Institute; Democracy South; Louisiana Legislative Black Caucus; National NAACP Office of the General Counsel; NAACP Legal Defense Fund (LDF); Norfolk State University; One Voice; the Southern Coalition for Social Justice (SCSJ) and the Young Elected Officials (YEO) Network.

Several notable consulting projects have highlighted Mr. Fairfax's career, including working as an expert to provide redistricting plans, research, and analysis for several court cases. Encompassed in his consulting portfolio is testifying in a federal redistricting court case as an expert witness. In addition, during the 2010 round of redistricting, he worked as the project director and consulting demographer for the Congressional Black Caucus Institute (CBC Institute). Ten years prior during the 2000 redistricting cycle, he was the CBC Institute's consulting demographer as well.

Mr. Fairfax is a graduate of Virginia Tech with a Bachelor of Science degree in electrical engineering. He is married to Dr. Colita Nichols Fairfax and has two daughters, Layla and Natalie.

PREFACE

It has been over a decade since I first discovered the phenomenon that is detailed in this book. Since then, what started as a series of modest questions has ended up as a full-blown political theory. In fact, the original theory has evolved over the past two presidential election cycles. Some of my original hypotheses have been modified or even eliminated and replaced by many more compelling ones. The theory has gone through a developmental process that has moved from a simple observation and a series of questions to quantifiable evidence. I firmly believe that the theory put forth in this book has the potential of changing the way presidential politics will be viewed for the next few decades or until another major political realignment occurs.

At the core of the theory lies a major political trend that existed for almost three decades. For nearly 30 years, our country's electorate exhibited the effects of a major political realignment that mostly went undetected. One of the consequences of this realignment is an unknown phenomenon pertaining to the popular vote for president. This extraordinary occurrence is detailed in this book and is deemed *the presidential trend.* The book describes the cause of the phenomenon, measures its predictability, and outlines the future effects.

The structure of this book is divided into five distinct sections. Part One of the book includes chapters that describe the trend as well as discuss the historic environment that existed in order to create the predictable trend. Part Two includes chapters with statistical techniques that prove the presence of the trend and other observable theories. Part Three analyzes the trend at the state and local level. Part Four reviews exit poll data and compares it to the trend. Part Five includes chapters that outline the future potential results regarding the popular vote for the candidates running for president.

Those who do not desire to be inundated with statistics, but desire to obtain a synopsis of the book, should read the first chapter of the book. This chapter presents the reader with a chronological narrative of the discovery and theory development of the phenomenon and acts as a condensed version of the majority of the book. The first chapter is designed to act as a summary of the entire trend theory with much of the statistical analysis and longer descriptive evidence. The remaining chapters in Part One of the book are more descriptive and less data-driven. The descriptive portions are contained in the first several chapters (Chaps. 1 through 6). Nevertheless, those who wish to dust off the old stats book (or crack open a new one) may find Parts Two through Four, the statistics chapters (Chaps. 7 through 13), interesting along with the data supplied in the appendices. Finally, those who are interested in the future of the trend and its effect on the major political parties should enjoy Part Five, the final chapters of the book (Chaps. 14 through 15).

It is important to note that this book discusses the trend that occurred at the presidential level. It does not address any voting phenomenon that may have occurred at any other lower level of political office. As a result, the purpose of this book is to present and discuss a unique and possibly unknown trend pertaining to the popular vote for the Democratic candidate for president.

PART 1

The Phenomenon

Chapter 1

A Summary of the Presidential Trend

Introduction

What if there is a trend that practically no one knows about, yet it once had an impact on everyone in the United States? As unbelievable as it sounds, this is the case. This unique trend has existed in the US voting electorate and has gone unnoticed. Because this major occurrence seems to remain unknown and continue to shape current and future elections, it deserves some type of literary focus and debate. Instead of writing a purely academic publication, this first chapter is intentionally written so that the general public can read, understand, and appreciate the significance of the occurrence. Hence the primary reason for the story format of this summary chapter. The goal is to attempt to take you through the same journey that I went through when uncovering this unique trend—without using too much technical jargon. Most of the statistical analysis and equations have been separated and placed in other sections of the book.

The Discovery

Just as most stories begin, let us start on the first day. That is to say, the first day that the trend was originally discovered. On that day I was sitting at my desk in Washington, DC, reviewing a series of data reports.[1]

The documents I was studying were US Census Bureau reports that outlined the results of several presidential elections. For some reason, I continued to glance back at a particular graph, which depicted votes cast; specifically, the popular vote for president by a major political party from 1972 to 2000. I had seen this graph before, or at least a similar one, but had never seen the pattern that was identified on that specific day.

---

[1] At the time, I was consulting on a project for a newly formed nonprofit organization called the CBC Institute.

Figure 1-1 contains a copy of the page and graph taken from the 2001 statistical abstract of the United States.

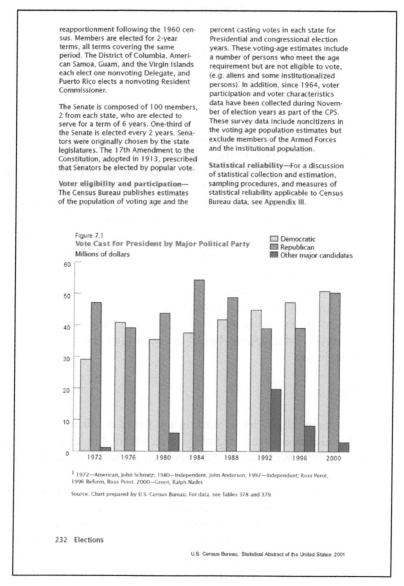

reapportionment following the 1960 census. Members are elected for 2-year terms, all terms covering the same period. The District of Columbia, American Samoa, Guam, and the Virgin Islands each elect one nonvoting Delegate, and Puerto Rico elects a nonvoting Resident Commissioner.

The Senate is composed of 100 members, 2 from each state, who are elected to serve for a term of 6 years. One-third of the Senate is elected every 2 years. Senators were originally chosen by the state legislatures. The 17th Amendment to the Constitution, adopted in 1913, prescribed that Senators be elected by popular vote.

Voter eligibility and participation— The Census Bureau publishes estimates of the population of voting age and the

percent casting votes in each state for Presidential and congressional election years. These voting-age estimates include a number of persons who meet the age requirement but are not eligible to vote, (e.g. aliens and some institutionalized persons). In addition, since 1964, voter participation and voter characteristics data have been collected during November of election years as part of the CPS. These survey data include noncitizens in the voting age population estimates but exclude members of the Armed Forces and the institutional population.

Statistical reliability—For a discussion of statistical collection and estimation, sampling procedures, and measures of statistical reliability applicable to Census Bureau data, see Appendix III.

Figure 7.1
Vote Cast for President by Major Political Party
Millions of dollars

☐ Democratic
■ Republican
■ Other major candidates

[Bar chart with years 1972, 1976, 1980, 1984, 1988, 1992, 1996, 2000 on x-axis and values 0 to 60 on y-axis]

¹ 1972—American, John Schmitz; 1980—Independent, John Anderson; 1992—Independent; Ross Perot, 1996 Reform, Ross Perot. 2000—Green, Ralph Nader.

Source: Chart prepared by U.S. Census Bureau. For data, see Tables 378 and 379.

232   Elections

U.S. Census Bureau, Statistical Abstract of the United States: 2001

Source: US Census Bureau, Statistical Abstract of the United States: 2001, pg. 232. Typo was removed from the original page.

Figure 1-1 Votes Cast for President, US Statistical Abstract, 2001 (pg. 232) (1972 to 2000)

4

Take a look at the page. If you do not see the pattern, look at Fig. 1-2 and view a zoomed-in recreation of the same graph with votes cast for the Republican and other major candidates removed.

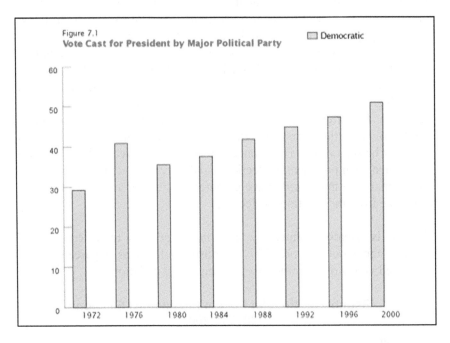

Source: US Census Bureau, Statistical Abstract of the United States: 2001, edited.

Figure 1-2 Popular Vote for Democratic Presidential Candidates
(1972 to 2000)

As you can clearly see, the popular vote for the Democratic candidate follows a straight line or *linear* trend from 1980 to 2000—a linear *presidential trend*. If you are wondering how straight or linear the trend was, review the second part of this book. In Part Two, statistical linear regression analysis is applied to determine how closely the trend follows a straight line. In fact, later it was discovered that the trend is so straight and predictable that the popular vote for the Democratic candidates for the elections of 1992, 1996, and 2000 could have been determined in 1988 with an accuracy of 99 percent or better (see Chap. 8 - Projecting the 1992 Election). In other words, Bill Clinton and Al Gore could have known their popular vote, within an error of 1 percent or less, almost

5

four years prior to their first presidential election run. As that previous statement sinks in, let me continue.

In some circumstances, a linear trend may not be an oddity. In fact, in many cases, we expect to see a linear trend. Most of us have seen linear trends in graphs that depict population growth. However, when I viewed the Republican popular vote over the same period of time, it seemingly showed no visible pattern at all (see Fig. 1-3). I say, "seemingly" because I found out later that there is a second, albeit more obscure pattern pertaining to the Republican and Independent candidates as well (see Chap. 4). To reiterate, at first it may seem that the Democratic linear trend should be the normal trend, and the Republican *fluctuating* votes cast may be the oddity. This stance can be quickly overturned when you realize that each presidential election had different turnout percentages of the popular vote that *should* have garnered fluctuating votes cast for each candidate from the election to election.

Turnout is usually defined by how many persons qualified to vote actually come out to vote. This is mostly defined as a percentage of registered voters or, in some cases, voting age population.

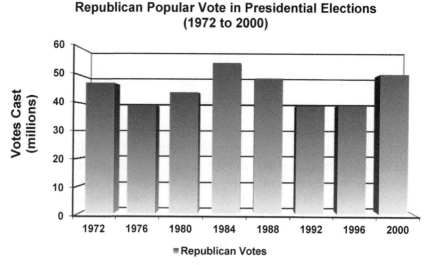

Source: US Census Bureau, Statistical Abstract of the United States: 2001

Figure 1-3 Republican Popular Vote
(1972 to 2000)

To illustrate, look at Fig. 1-4 and review the varying turnout percentages for the presidential elections from 1972 to 2000. In order for the growth of votes cast to increase in a straight line, there should have been a consistent turnout percentage or at least a steadily increasing pattern.

As Fig. 1-4 indicates, there seems to be no consistent linear pattern for the turnout percentage. The graph shows that, in some elections, there was an increase in the turnout from the previous election; in others there was a decrease. This makes perfect sense when considering the fact that a variety of different Republican and Democratic candidates, each with differing appeal, should garner different voter turnout.

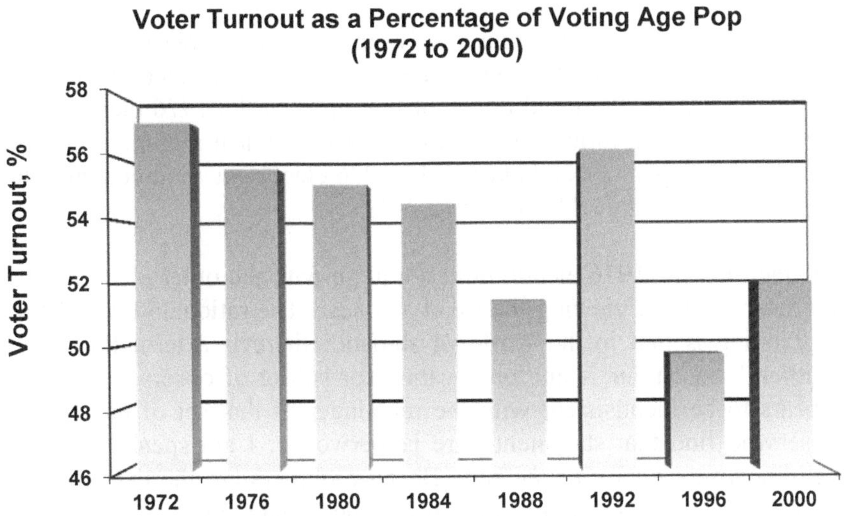

Voter Turnout as a Percentage of Voting Age Pop (1972 to 2000)

Source: US Census Bureau Statistical Abstract of the US, 2004 (Table HS-52)

Figure 1-4 Voter Turnout as a Percentage of Voting Age Population (1972 to 2000)

Consider the Republican candidates: Ronald Reagan, George H. W. Bush, Bob Dole, and George W. Bush. Now consider the Democratic candidates: Jimmy Carter, Walter Mondale, Michael Dukakis, Bill Clinton, and Al Gore. You can easily see that they encompassed different characteristics and thus should have garnered differing popular votes. In addition to different types of candidates, there were different current issues, different national and global economic conditions, and much more. These potential variations made the linear trend even more astounding.

Thus the Republican candidates' popular vote varied, and the overall turnout varied, but the Democratic candidates' popular vote consistently trended upward in a straight-line fashion. After considering the varying conditions from election to election, clearly, the oddity is the linear vote trend of the Democratic candidates and not the varying votes for the Republican candidates. This discrepancy between the Democratic popular vote and the Republican popular vote is baffling. Likewise, how can a linear trend exist when the turnout of voters and other factors varied from election to election?

Nevertheless, before attempting to solve that question, I observed that the trend from 1980 to 2000 seems to align itself with the election of 1972. At the same time, the trend does not line up with the 1976 election. To view the trend in a format that easily reveals the linear alignment, a new graph is developed. To add clarity, the 1976 election is removed, and the Republican votes are added (see Fig. 1-5).

The fact that the 1976 election did not align with the other elections did not deter me from viewing the trend as linear. The rationale for this line of thinking is that in the world of statistics there is a term known as "outlier." An outlier is an "observation (or subset of observations) that appears to be inconsistent with the remainder of that set of data."[2] For those who find that statement pure jabberwocky, I am speaking of the well-known *exception to the rule*. Because outliers are the exception to the rule, they are commonly discarded when analyzing a trend pattern. This did not mean that I would not seek to answer the question of what occurred in 1976 and why it was an outlier (see Chap. 3). However, the 1976 election is not included in the trend analysis for this book and *may* be one of the central reasons why other researchers have not discovered the trend.

---

[2] Vic Barnett, Toby Lewis, *Outliers in Statistical Data*, John & Wiley and Sons, 1994

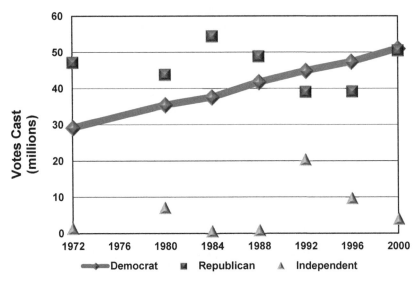

Source: U.S. Census Bureau, Statistical Abstract of the United States, 2001

Figure 1-5 Democratic, Republican, & Independent Popular Vote
(1972 to 2000, w/o 1976)

Figure 1-5 epitomized the uniqueness of the trend. That is to say that the Democratic popular vote increased in a linear fashion while the votes for the Republican and Independent candidates fluctuated. Within a relatively short period after discovering the trend, several questions needed to be answered, including:

1. When did the trend begin?
2. Why was the trend linear?
3. What caused the trend to be linear?
4. Was there additional proof that validated the trend?
5. What created the trend realignment?

With all of these questions on the table, I set out to research and address them one by one.

When Did the Trend Begin?

In order to unravel the genesis of the trend, there needed to be a review of the popular vote for elections prior to 1972. This review should assist with answering whether or not the trend began in 1972, or did it begin prior to that time?

The first step was to obtain the election results prior to 1972. I turned to two sources: the US Census Bureau and an excellent all-in-one website for past presidential, senatorial, and gubernatorial election results: Dave Leip's *Atlas of US Presidential Elections*[3].

Using the data obtained, several new graphs are created. The first graph shows the popular vote for the Democratic candidates from 1940 to 2000 (see Fig. 1-6). I felt that 1940 is far enough in the past to allow the origin of the trend to appear.

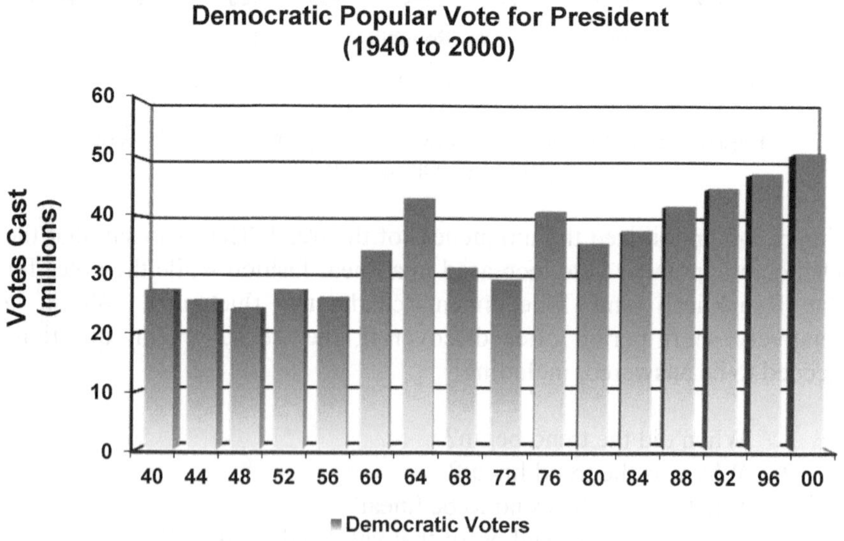

**Democratic Popular Vote for President
(1940 to 2000)**

Source: US Census Bureau Statistical Abstracts 1942 to 2001 and uselectionatlas.org

Figure 1-6 Popular Vote for Democratic Presidential Candidates
(1940 to 2000)

---

[3] Although the Census Bureau had much of the required information, Leip's website consolidated data into a readily usable format.

As the figure shows, there is no visible indication of a linear trend prior to 1972.[4] For comparison sake, a graph of the Republican candidates' popular vote from 1940 to 2000 is created (see Fig. 1-7). Once again, there is no visible consistent linear trend prior to or after 1972.[5]

Therefore, the second question has been solved. The trend seems to begin in 1972. A second question may be lingering in your mind, "When did the trend end?" The short answer is that the trend ended in 2000. However, it would take more than a sentence or two to explain *what occurred* after the trend ended. The analysis of what occurred after the trend is presented in Part 4 of this book. Nonetheless, on to solving the *cause of the linear trend.*

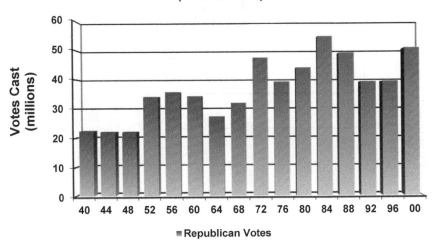

Republican Popular Vote for President (1940 to 2000)

Source: US Census Bureau Statistical Abstracts 1942 to 2001 and uselectionatlas.org

Figure 1-7 Popular Vote for Republican Presidential Candidates (1940 to 2000)

---

[4] There is a peculiar voting consistency for 1940, 1944, and 1948 for the Democratic and Republican candidate that may be researched at a later date.
[5] Some political analysts believe that a realignment began in 1964.

Why Is the Trend Linear?

One of the central underlining questions of this book is what caused the popular vote for the Democratic candidates to be linear? Of course, this required an initial assumption that a trend such as this would *not* have occurred during the natural election cycles. There had to be some unique circumstance for the popular vote of the Democratic candidates to align itself in a straight line while the popular vote for the Republican candidate varied from election to election. In addition, there is one more assumption: something *substantial* must have transpired prior to or during the 1972 election cycle in order for the linear trend to occur. As I went through various scenarios of how the popular vote increased in a steadily predictable pattern, I came across a previously created graph that gave me a clue (see Fig. 1-8).

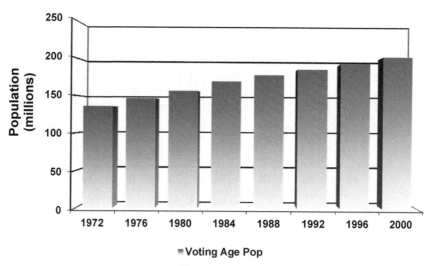

Voting Age Population in Presidential Elections (1972 to 2000)

Source: US Census Bureau, Reported Voting Rates in Presidential Election Years, by Selected Characteristics: November 1964 to 2004

Figure 1-8 Voting Age Population in Pres. Elections
(1972 to 2000)

The graph depicts the increase in voting age population (VAP) from 1972 to 2000 elections. The voting age population is made up of persons above the age of 18 years.[6]

The graph of the VAP is so similar to the graph of the popular vote for the Democratic candidate that I contemplated if there is a connection between the two. After some reflection, I concluded that the connection is that, similar to the VAP, the trend shows the *linear* increase in voting population. To some readers, this may seem like an logical connection to make, but bear with me as I attempt to elaborate on why this is important.[7]

It was expected that the popular vote would increase as the voting age population increased. However, the caveat is that the trend seems to *only* show an increase in turnout of the voting population. The emphasis is on the *only*. This means that other factors had *not* noticeably influenced the popular vote for the Democratic candidate—except the increase in the voting population.[8] This includes factors such as different election turnout percentages, candidates, current domestic situation, or global conditions. Just about any other aspect that you can think of did *not* seem to have an impact on the votes cast for the Democratic candidate (other than the growth in voting population).[9] My belief is that if those factors had considerably influenced votes cast, there would have been evidence by the significant fluctuation of the popular vote.

After some contemplation, I determined that the popular vote for the Democratic candidate during this trend period consists of three major groups of voters:

---

[6] Prior to 1972, some states minimum voting age was older than 21 years or even more.

[7] Registered voters and specifically the turnout of those voters is the true measurement of the increase in voters from election to election.

[8] To demonstrate how well the Democratic votes cast related to the overall VAP from 1972 to 2000 (excluding 1976), the ratio of the Democratic popular vote to VAP varies from only 21.4 to 25.2 percent (3.8 percent) while the Republican popular vote to VAP varies from 20.2 to 34.6 percent (14.4 percent).

[9] I later discovered that the trend associated with the total voting age population is less even linear than the Democratic trend.

1) Persons who voted for the Democratic candidate in the previous election;

2) Persons who previously voted for the Republican or Independent Party's candidates in the previous election;

3) Persons who were first-time voters or did not vote in the previous election.

Here resides the beginning of the basis for what I called *the presidential trend theory*. My hypothesis is that the first category, which included voters who previously voted for the Democratic candidate, made up the bulk of the voters in each election. At a lesser extent, the remaining voters came from the second and third categories of voters. These additional voters included those who *swung over* to vote for the Democratic candidate from Republican and Independent candidates and first-time voters or ones who did not vote in the previous election. The assumption is that if the second group of voters was significant, the swing voters, the trend should have fluctuated significantly from election to election. In addition, if the number of voters in the swing group were *consistent* from election to election, it could be a larger population. This turned out to be the case (see Chap. 13).

Just as the VAP trend is linear because it consists of essentially current persons above the age of 18 plus an increase in a new group of persons who just became 18, the vote for the Democratic candidate is similar. Once more, the popular vote for the Democratic candidate is linear because it consists mostly of voters who previously voted for the Democratic candidate plus new *first-time* voters also voting for the Democratic candidate. The final additional types of voters include voters who did not vote in the previous presidential election plus swing voters.

Armed with this new theory, I needed to find a relatively quick way to confirm the hypothesis before moving further into developing a complete theory. The quick solution to verifying the hypothesis is simple and straightforward. Essentially, if the Democratic popular vote consisted of mostly the previous Democratic voters[10] plus new first-time voters, then

---

[10] The use of Democratic voters throughout this book refers to voters who vote for the Democratic candidate in the particular election analyzed.

the popular vote for a particular election could be *estimated* using these two items. Therefore, a simple check is to add the previous Democratic popular vote plus new first-time voters and compare the sum with actual results. If the results of this crude analysis are accurate, analysis that is more detailed could be delved into more deeply.

Data were gathered to test the hypothesis. The previous popular vote data were already available; however, first-time voter information needed to be obtained from exit polls. In this specific case, the 1972 and 1980 elections should *not* be estimated using the same technique. Both of the previous elections, 1968 and 1976, respectively, were not appropriate to use.

As previously mentioned, the election of 1976 was an anomaly, an extraordinary amount of voters voted for the Democratic candidate. The abundance of Democratic voters would certainly skew the estimate. The election of 1968 had a different problem. First-time voter data for this election is not available. Even if it were available, this election occurred prior to the completion of the electoral fracturing. Therefore neither the 1972 nor 1980 election would be appropriate to use for this particular estimation and verification technique.

In order to calculate the popular vote for the 1984 to 2000 elections, percentage of first-time voters, and partisan portion of those voters, the number of first-time voters for each party designation is estimated. An accuracy of the estimate is derived by comparing the estimate to the actual Democratic votes cast.[11] Chapter 4 details the formulas that use exit polls to estimate the popular vote using first-time voters.

As Table 1-1 indicates, the accuracy of adding the previous popular vote plus the estimated number of first-time voters for the Democratic candidates is no less than 95.7 percent with an average of 97.5 percent. When the same accuracy check is calculated for the Republican candidates, the accuracy is as low as 69.9 percent with an average of 83.8 percent.

---

[11] Although not displayed, the 1980 popular vote was used in the calculations for the 1984 estimates.

Viewing the results from Table 1-1, the Democratic candidate's popular vote appears to be very close estimates. The estimates for Republican candidates are not as accurate and fluctuate from election to election. The stunning accuracy and consistency of the estimates for the Democratic popular vote using the previous election plus the first-time voters is another strong piece of evidence validating the initial theory of the presidential trend. Nevertheless, further detailed analysis of the makeup of the Democratic electorate reveals a more complex configuration (see Chap. 13).

Table 1-1 Estimate of First-time Voters & Accuracy of Popular Vote Estimate, 1984 to 2000

	1984	1988	1992	1996	2000
First-Time Democratic Voters (Mil)	2.8	3.0	2.9	4.7	4.9
First-Time Republican Voters (Mil)	4.5	3.3	2.0	2.9	4.1
First-Time Independents Voters (Mil)			1.4	1.0	0.4
Total Democratic Voters Actual (Mil)	37.6	41.8	44.9	47.4	51.0
Total Democratic Voters est. (Mil)	38.3	40.6	44.7	49.6	52.3
Accuracy of Democratic est., %	98.1	97.1	99.5	95.4	97.4
Total Republican Voters Actual (Mil)	54.5	48.9	39.1	39.2	50.5
Total Republican Voters est. (Mil)	48.4	57.7	50.9	42.1	43.3
Accuracy of Republican est., %	88.9	81.9	69.9	92.7	85.8

Sources: *New York Times* exit polls (1980 to 2000); US Census Bureau Statistical Abstracts 2001

Although the table clearly shows a high accuracy rate for the projected amount of Democratic candidate's votes, it is still astounding and tends to disagree with conventional political theory. However, once again, there is one vital stipulation. These voters who formed the trend do so in presidential elections. Elections at other levels (congressional, gubernatorial, etc.) may not display aspects of the presidential trend.[12] In other words, these unique voters form a trend when voting in presidential elections *only*. The fact that this trend may only be visible or even present at the presidential level could be another reason why it has not been discovered thus far. Some analysts lump all voters together despite

---

[12] I do believe that this trend, at the presidential level, is the preverbal "canary in the coal mine." In other words, as our electorate becomes increasingly polarized, we could see the trend eventually manifest itself at lower levels.

the type of elections (e.g., a Democratic voter in presidential elections is a Democratic voter in gubernatorial elections). In order to view this trend, and possibly others, only presidential elections should be analyzed.

I also came to realize that these old and new Democratic voters voted fairly consistently. Simply put, if they did not vote much of the time, the trend would *not* have been linear. The popular vote for the Democratic candidate would have acted similarly to the popular vote for the Republican candidate. It would have fluctuated up and down with the turnout of voters. It did not. Nonetheless, as stated above, an analysis of various exit poll data reveals that the Democratic voters may have crossed over more than the actual results indicated.

That being said, evidence points to the Democratic voters consistently voting from election to election. However, it is important to *not* minimize what it took to ensure that these voters continued to vote in each presidential election. Since the early eighties, the Democrats have had an exceptional voter registration and get out the vote (GOTV) effort in to order to ensure that Democratic voters, specifically the party's base voters, continue to add to the pool of voters and turn out to vote. [13] Without these efforts, the Democratic popular vote may have fluctuated. Therefore, the Democratic Party's exceptional voter registration or GOTV efforts may be *one* of the reasons why the trend has been sustained for so long.

Therefore, the answer to this second question is determined. The trend is linear because the popular vote for the Democratic presidential candidate consisted of mostly voters who previously voted for the Democratic candidate plus a new batch of voters. Each new election cycle continued the pattern of previous Democratic voters plus a new batch of new voters.

Even though the majority of voters were made up of previous democratic voter and new voters, there was a group of voters who swung back and forth between the Democratic candidates and the Republican or Independent candidates. The hypothesis for these voters is that they

---

[13] Hundreds of progressive civic engagement organizations that tend to focus on the underserved communities contributed to increasing and turning out the base. These organizations add to the millions of new registrants and motivate the base to vote.

constitute either a small amount or the amount of voters are relatively consistent from election to election. After exit poll analysis, it is determined that these swing voters are relatively stable (see Chap. 13). The swing voters, which are a smaller amount, are fairly consistent. Hence, after 1972, the popular vote for the Democratic candidate for president consists of these three groups and thus increases in a linear fashion, excluding the election of 1976.

What Causes the Trend To Be Linear?

The final *critical* question to the development of the theory is the most difficult to answer. The previous question addresses the *why* of the trend. This question, which seems like the same question, focuses on the *what*. What happened to the electorate in order for this linear trend to occur?

This question had been nagging me from the very beginning. However, the previous questions had to be answered in order to answer this fundamental one. I now had several components of this analytical puzzle in place, with one big hole in the middle. The pieces of the puzzle already established include:

1) No visible indication of the trend prior to 1972 (from 1940 to 1972);

2) A linear trend of the Democratic popular vote began in 1972 and continued to the year 2000 (excluding 1976);

3) The Democratic popular vote from 1972 to 2000 consisted mostly of the Democratic voters who previously voted for the Democratic candidate and new Democratic voters voting for the first time; and

4) The Democratic voters tended to vote consistently (possibly due to the continued voter engagement efforts).

I approached solving this new question by solving a simpler question: Why did the Democratic popular vote only contain essentially Democratic voters after 1972? The general answer to this question is easy. Something had to occur to the electorate to cause only the Democratic voters to vote for the Democratic candidate. Furthermore, whatever happened had to be substantial and had to affect the entire national electorate. In order to determine what occurred, I had to view the electorate in a unique manner.

Understanding that there had been other times in our electoral history where voting behavior changed, I began reviewing past types of voting trends or analysis (see Chap. 3 for details). I discovered a couple of unique political analysts. One analyst, Valdimer Orlando Key (V.O. Key), pioneered viewing voter behavior attributes and election results to analyze elections. The other analyst, Louis H. Bean, used the country's economic conditions to predict election outcome.

Nonetheless, part of Louis Bean's theory, as well as others, centers on a particular voting trend analogy. This analogy centered on the assumption that certain conditions in our country occur where one political party comes into power like a *tidal wave* coming onto shore.[14] That party would remain in power for a particular period of time.[15] Then, just like tidal waves that roll back out to sea, so would the party's control. Each time this tidal wave occurred, analysts felt that a new political *realignment* also occurred. However, the presidential trend incorporated realignment is different from the tidal wave theory. The tidal wave theory does not fully explain the linear trending phenomenon, so I was compelled to expand on this and other similar theories to develop a new one.

At this point, I started this new theory with a central assumption. Since it was shown that the Democratic popular vote was mostly the previous Democratic popular vote plus first-time voters, the assumption is that after 1972, the Democratic popular vote consisted of essentially core Democratic voters. These core voters consisted of voters who had a high propensity to vote for the Democratic candidate. The core voters did not need much or if any persuasion to vote for the Democratic candidate. It is important to *not* confuse persuasion with motivation to turnout. The fact that they were core voters does not mean that they did not require motivation to turn out. The Democratic candidates still required efforts to turn these core voters out and vote.

---

[14] Louis Bean, who predicted the win by Truman against Dewey in 1948, has been credited for developing the concept of *political cycles* or *political tides*.
[15] Usually the realignments last between 30 to 40 years.

However, once the core voter assumption is made, it is quickly realized that if these voters had become the only voters voting for the Democratic candidate, they might as well have been voting in a separate electorate— essentially all by themselves. In fact, in order to understand this rationale for the trend, our presidential electorate has to be viewed, not as one, but as *two separate electorates*. I conclude that, somehow, the presidential electorate had been *fractured* into at least two pieces. A later discovery showed that the electorate did not completely fracture (see Chap. 13). In reality, a portion of the electorate remained connected together for a relatively minor group of voters who switched (or swung) back and forth from electorate to electorate. Yet, in order to understand what had occurred, this unique theoretical model needed to be simplified and viewed as if the electorate at the presidential level had been completely broken apart.

Consequently, the first portion of the fractured electorate had already been established. It contained mostly the core Democratic voters. This portion of only Democratic voters explains the existence of the linear trend. This new theoretical electorate only contained voters who tended to vote for the Democratic candidate plus a consistent amount of new Democratic voters yielded a linear trend for the popular vote.

Therefore, the first fractured portion is titled, the "Democratic Electorate" since it mostly contains Democratic voters (see Fig. 1-9). The second portion that shows no linear trend for the popular vote, and includes everyone else, is titled the "Non-Democratic Electorate."

To those who would think it should be called the "Republican Electorate," this simply is not accurate. This second electorate contained voters who mostly voted for the Republican candidate and also included a sizable amount of voters who did not. Proof of this determination will be presented later in this chapter and other chapters of this book. Given that the voters included in the second fractured part of the electorate did not or hardly ever vote for the Democratic presidential candidate, this part is given the name "Non-Democratic Electorate".

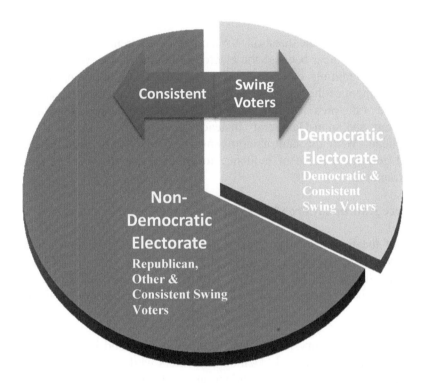

Figure 1-9 Graphical Representation of the Fractured Electorate Post 1972

Therefore the question, "Why did the Democratic candidates' popular vote only or mostly contain the core voters after 1972?" is answered. The answer is that our voting electorate at the presidential level has been fractured into two pieces. One piece contains mainly voters who voted for the Democratic candidate.[16] The other part contains mainly voters

---

[16] Expanding this line of thinking, the trend could be viewed from a pure sense as both a minimum and a maximum (or ceiling) of votes cast for the Democratic candidate for president. Viewing this trend as a *minimum*, the Democratic candidates voters were mostly base or core voters who voted for the Democratic candidate most of the time. Hence the votes should not go below a minimum amount of votes. Viewing the fractured electorate as a *maximum* depends on the circumstance whereby the Democratic candidate is unable to access a significant

who voted for the Republican candidate, in addition to the voters who, voted for Independent candidates.

Thus, the answer to the question, "What causes the trend to be linear?" is answered. It is linear because the electorate fractured into two parts with one part containing chiefly Democratic voters. In addition, another critical element of the presidential trend theory had been established. The electorate at the presidential level should be primarily viewed in terms of Democrat and non-Democrat instead of the usual Democrat and Republican. With the central components of the theory established, I sought additional proof or evidence to validate that the electorate had been fractured.

Is There Additional Proof That Validates the Trend?

Proof of the linear trend is undeniable. There is no doubt that a linear trend existed for the Democratic candidates' popular vote from 1972 to 2000 (excluding 1976). However, given the dramatic nature of this brand-new theory, additional proof that the electorate had been fractured is needed.

To reiterate, the theory is that the electorate is fractured into two parts: one essentially includes only Democratic voters while the other, the non-Democratic side, includes Republican and Independent voters (see Fig. 1-9). There is an assumption that there still existed a small portion of each electorate that crossed over, but this is not a major amount. Thus, if the electorate for the most part had truly been fractured, with the result being the linear trend, what other evidence other than the trend could be visible due to this fracturing? Could there have been some other trend or trends created due to the fracturing? Thus, I set out to consider each electorate separately and attempt to discover additional proof that validated the fractured electorate.

To verify the Democratic side, proof is needed to show that this portion of the electorate contained only one set of voters. These were voters who essentially voted only for the Democratic candidates. I imagine that if the electorate was fractured, the Democratic candidates were isolated from

---

amount of the voters in the non-Democratic electorate. Hence the votes constituted a maximum of votes obtained by the Democratic candidates.

the voters that vote for the Republican or other Independent candidates. It is considered that, since there were only voters voting for the Democratic candidate in this portion of the electorate, there should be some evidence of votes cast for the Democratic candidates *not* being affected by the votes for the Republican or Independent candidates, or even both.

This assumption relies on the fact that in normal elections, one candidate usually pulls votes away from the other candidate. However, if there are only voters voting for a *single* candidate there should be no pulling away of these votes. This means that there should be no decrease in the Democratic candidates votes with an increase in votes for Republican, Independent Party candidates or both.

Therefore, the votes for the Democratic candidates need to be compared with the ones for Republican and then with the ones for the Independent candidates. If these two are plotted on a line graph, there should be a visible dip in the graph of one candidate's votes with the increase in the other. If this increase and dip relationship is visible, it will be an indication that there was a *pulling* away of votes from one candidate to another. If there is no dipping, this should tend to validate that the two were isolated from each other.

The Democratic and Republican candidate graphs are created in Fig. 1.5. Reviewing this graph, in a similar format, the chart reveals that there is no noticeable effect of one candidate pulling votes away from the other (see Figure 1-10).

Under normal circumstances, votes cast for the Republican candidates should have had some effect on the Democratic candidates' votes or vice versa. Clearly, the graph shows none. Excited with the results of the first test, I plotted the Democratic and Independent party's candidates' votes to determine if there was any effect on one another. Again, since the Democratic electorate contained only votes for the Democratic candidate, there should not be any effect of the votes cast for the other major party candidates on the Democratic candidates or vice versa.

As Fig. 1-11 shows, once again there is no noticeable effect. These two graphs tend to validate the theory that the Democratic side only contains voters who voted for the Democratic candidates. Plainly, these two charts show additional evidence that the Democratic Electorate is isolated from the Republican and Independent candidate's voters.

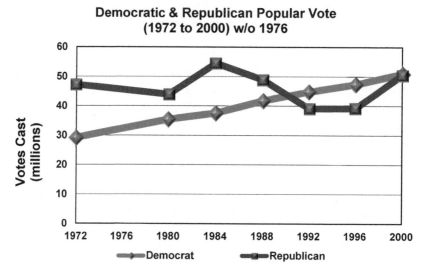

Sources: US Census Bureau Statistical Abstracts 1942 to 2001 and uselectionatlas.org

Figure 1-10 Democratic & Republican Popular Vote
(1972 to 2000, w/o 1976)

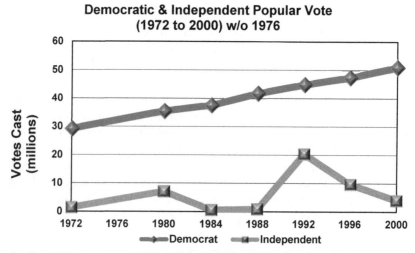

Sources: US Census Bureau Statistical Abstracts 1942 to 2001 and uselectionatlas.org

Figure 1-11 Democratic & Independent Popular Vote
(1972 to 2000, w/o 1976)

Armed with this proof of the isolation for the Democratic electorate, I considered, "What would the other side of the fractured electorate show?" In the theoretical other electorate, the non-Democratic side, there were essentially two types of voters. They included those who voted for the Republican candidates and those who voted for Independent candidates.

The method used to validate that the Democratic electorate contained *one* type of voter was to show that the Democratic candidate's votes were not affected by the Republican or Independent candidates. For the non-Democratic electorate, a different method has to be devised that would show evidence that *two* types of candidates were contained in the second electorate. I looked for a voting pattern that reflected the existence of only two categories of candidates; in other words, almost the opposite of the Democratic Electorate. The pattern should reflect two types of candidates or parties directly *pulling* voters away from the other. There is one quick notation on Independent candidates. This analysis and others in this book relies on lumping all of the Independent candidates into one category type.[17]

The method developed for the purpose of verifying that only two categories of voters were contained in the electorate is to detect a symmetrical or inverse relationship or what could be called the "mirror effect." To illustrate the *ideal* mirror effect, I created the graph in Fig. 1-12, which depicts a simple two-party race. The graph clearly shows a unique pattern, which creates a *mirroring* or symmetrical pattern of the two different party's votes.

The reason why the mirror image existed was due to the two candidates vying for the same voters. The two combined make up the total votes counted. In the example, if 60 voters turned out to vote, and one party received 47 votes, then the other party must have received 13 votes. If one party received 45 votes, then the other party must have received only 15 votes. Essentially, one party received a certain amount of votes while the other received the remaining amount. This example of the ideal mirroring assumes 60 total voters for each election and more importantly, every voter voted. If the turnout of total votes fluctuated, the *ideal* mirror

---

[17] There is recognition that some Independent voters were diametrically opposed to each other. However, they represent a small amount of the total voters and do not affect the overall analysis.

pattern is not produced. This of course is what occurs under realistic conditions. Therefore, there should never be an exact mirror image under true electoral conditions. Nonetheless, if the results plotted on a graph show a propensity of mirroring of one party to the other, it should be a great indicator of the presence of only two parties.

Example of Mirroring of Votes Cast for Two Party Races

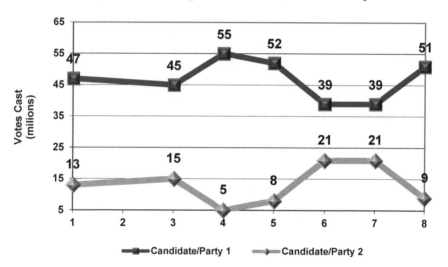

Figure 1-12 Example of Mirroring Votes Cast for Two-Party Races

Consequently, I thought that if I could find a pattern similar to the one shown in Fig. 1-12, then that would be evidence that only two categories existed in the non-Democratic electorate and additional evidence of the fracturing of our electorate. It also would validate the rationalization for labeling this electorate the non-Democratic electorate instead of the Republican electorate.

As a result, I plotted the votes cast for the Republican and the sum of all the Independent Party candidates on a graph. As before, I was astonished when I saw the graph images of Fig. 1-13. It shows a distinct mirroring of Republican and Independent candidates' votes.

Nevertheless, as you can see, the result is not two perfectly symmetrical images, though a mirroring of each line graph is clearly visible. First, the total votes cast for Republican and Independent candidates fluctuate from election to election. This is unlike the ideal situation depicted in

Figure 1-12, which includes the same vote total. Second, there are actually three options for voters in the non-Democratic Electorate: 1) vote for the Republican candidate; 2) vote for one of the Independent Party candidates; or 3) not vote at all. The third option could be the reason why the image of the votes for the Republican candidate and the combined votes for the Independent Party candidates do not perfectly mirror each other. Most likely there was an election whereby the voters either turned out at a higher than usual rate or simply did not vote. This would be reflected on the graph.

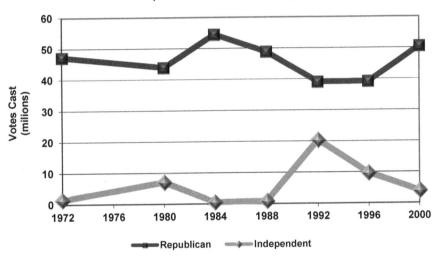

Republican & Independent Popular Vote
(1972 to 2000 w/o 1976)

Sources: US Census Bureau Statistical Abstracts 1942 to 2001 and uselectionatlas.org

Figure 1-13 Republican & Independent Popular Vote
(1972 to 2000, w/o 1976)

The point on the graph that does *not* produce a mirror effect as much as the other elections occurs in 1992. It seems that during that year, the leading Independent Party candidate, Ross Perot, distorts the mirroring pattern by performing exceptionally well. However, it is the result of the Republican candidate, George H. W. Bush, in the election of 1992 and 1996 that led me to contemplate another associated pattern of the trend theory, which is covered in Chap. 6.

What Created the Trend Realignment?

Probably the question with the most provocative and controversial answer is the question of "What created or promoted the trend realignment?" This is to say, did the Democratic Party provoke voters to move away from voting for its candidates? Alternatively, did the Republicans or Independent candidates offer something that shifted voters toward their candidates? They each sound similar, yet there is a subtle difference between the two.

My hypothesis is that voters moved away from the Democratic presidential candidates or party. The key to this hypothesis is Independent voters. The voters' focal point of the fracturing seemed to be the Democratic candidates. It was as if a portion of the country's voters were determined to vote for anyone except the Democratic candidates. Although there is evidence that there was some crossover from Democratic electorate to the non-Democratic electorate the amount seemed relatively small.

Thus, the Independent voters and possibly some Republican voters made a conscience decision to shift away from the Democratic candidates and party. In order for this to occur, those voters must have disagreed with Democratic policies or initiatives so much that this portion of the electorate would not vote for the Democratic candidate for the next 30 years or more (excluding 1976).

With this hypothesis established, research could begin on what occurred to create the trend. Since the trend began in 1972, the natural starting point is the review that election. In that election, the Democratic candidate was Senator George S. McGovern and the Republican was President Richard M. Nixon, who was seeking his second term. Nixon won in what would be considered a landslide. He won 49 states to McGovern's one state and the District of Columbia. McGovern's platform included a fundamental issue: ending the Vietnam War[18]. On the other hand, Nixon also promised that peace was nearing in Vietnam by continuing to implement his policies. Because both sides were touting that they would end the war, the Vietnam War could not have been the

---

[18] McGovern also promised to institute programs that would guarantee income to the nation's poor.

major occurrence that fractured the electorate in two pieces. Vietnam may have played some type of role, just not the dominant one.

McGovern was also labeled by Nixon as "too liberal for the country." Nixon reinforced a statement by Senator Thomas Eagleton that McGovern is for "Amnesty, Abortion and Acid." [19] Under normal circumstances that statement may not have been unusual. However, Eagleton just happened to have been selected as McGovern's vice presidential candidate. Later, McGovern fired Eagleton and selected Sargent Shriver as his running mate. Nonetheless, this liberal label attached to McGovern was not enough to fracture the voting electorate and establish a trend for the next three decades. Once again, the liberal aspect of the Democratic candidate played a role in the fracturing, just not the primary one.

After reviewing the events of the 1972 election, no evidence was substantial enough to fracture the electorate. As I continued to research, I recalled that the presidential election of 1968 was considered by some political analysts to be a "realigning election."[20] The election ended the dominance by the Democratic Party that began with Franklin D. Roosevelt in 1932.[21] In fact, an aide to Richard Nixon, Kevin P. Phillips, wrote that after the 1968 election, *realignment* occurred whereby the southern region of the country would ultimately become Republican.[22] Therefore, I contemplated, *What if the trend began in 1972, but the fracturing actually occurred in 1968?*

What came to mind about the 1968 election was that it exemplified the decade of sixties. In fact, some call the sixties the "turbulent sixties" (see Chap. 2). Throughout the sixties, there was a growing divide in the country due to several polarizing issues such as the increase in recreational drug use; a new sexual revolution; the women's liberation movement; a prolonged war in Vietnam; and of course civil rights. The unique aspect of most of these major issues in the sixties was that they

---

[19] *Time* magazine, August 1972 issue, "The Eagleton Affair."
[20] The shear existence of the trend confirms the reality of some type of realignment.
[21] Franklin Roosevelt's New Deal shifted millions of Republican voters to become Democratic voters.
[22] Nicol C. Rae, *Southern Democrat*, Oxford University Press, 1994

were all dividing the country into *liberal* and *conservative* groups. Consequently, this growing division of our society was literally segmenting the population and at the same time dividing our electorate into two sides. With the convolution of these divergent issues, our country and electorate was literally being stretched throughout the sixties to a breaking point. It was simply a matter of time before one of the issues became a catalyst for a major electoral realignment.

In 1968, Dr. Martin Luther King Jr. and Robert Kennedy were assassinated; race riots proliferated throughout the country; violence occurred at the 1968 Democratic convention; and there were widespread protests against the Vietnam war. Politically, thanks to these events, along with the fact that President Lyndon Johnson decided not to seek an additional term, the Democratic Party and much of its voting electorate were left somewhat in disarray.

Since the Democratic Party had no clear-cut succession of leadership, some scholars believe the 1968 convention, which was designed to choose a presidential candidate and leader, was divided into several factions[23]:

1) Big-city party bosses, led by Mayor Richard J. Daily of Chicago, Illinois. This faction supported Senator Hubert Humphrey;

2) Followers of Senator Eugene McCarthy who were comprised mostly of activist against the Vietnam War;

3) Catholics, African Americans, and other racial and ethnic minorities. These individuals were rallying behind Senator Robert Kennedy; and

4) White Southern Democrats or (former) Dixiecrats. Some members supported Hubert Humphrey; however, most of them would end up supporting George C. Wallace from Alabama.

The particular faction that stands out to me is the fourth group, which consisted mostly of white Southern Democrats. As you may recall,

---

[23] Phillip E. Converse, Warren E. Miller, Jerrold G. Rusk, Arthur C. Wolfe, *Continuity and Change in American Politics: Parties and Issues in the 1968 Election*, 1969; Wikipedia, *United States Presidential Election, 1968*

Alabama's George C. Wallace *split* [24] from the Democratic Party to lead the charge to join and expand the American Independent Party. In 1968, George Wallace received over 9.9 million votes or 13.5 percent of the popular vote. This was the largest third-party vote total since 1924. [25]

As a quick refresher, several years before (in 1962), Wallace was elected governor of Alabama on a pro-segregation, pro-states' rights platform. He won a landslide victory. At that time, he gave his most infamous speech, which included:

> "In the name of the greatest people that have ever trod this earth, I draw the line in the dust and toss the gauntlet before the feet of tyranny, and I say segregation now, segregation tomorrow, segregation forever."

In 1963, Wallace made news again by standing in front of the auditorium at the University of Alabama in order to stop two black students, Vivian Malone and James Hood, from enrolling. Using his public image, Wallace ran, albeit unsuccessfully, for the Democratic nomination for president in 1964. In the 1968 election, his prior words and track record still resonated with many voters. Wallace and the American Independent Party vehemently opposed the 1964 Civil Rights Act. It was not that they simply opposed the 1964 Civil Rights Act; they opposed federal efforts to end desegregation, including opposition to the 1965 Voting Rights Act and the 1968 Civil Rights Act (also known as the Fair Housing Act). The Civil Rights Act of 1964 prohibited discrimination in public facilities and certain employment practices; the Voting Rights Act of 1965 prohibited discriminatory practices in voting, and the Civil Rights Act of 1968 outlawed discrimination in the sale or rental of housing.

The statement that President Johnson purportedly made to his press secretary after signing the Civil Rights Act was prophetic: "I think we have just delivered the South to the Republican Party for a long time to come." Johnson instinctively felt that a portion of the country, specifically the South, was not ready for the change that was about to

---

[24] I later determined that the term "split-off" is a perfect description of what occurred.

[25] In 1924, Republican Robert M. La Follette received 4,831,706 votes for 16.6 percent of the popular vote in the Progressive Party.

occur due to the enacted civil rights legislation. He knew that, although polls indicated a majority of the country tended to favor the Civil Rights Act, there was a population in the country that adamantly opposed it. For instance, 62 percent of those surveyed in the Harris Poll of April 1964 stated they favored such a law. Similar findings were made regarding the Voting Rights Act. A Gallup poll taken in the spring of 1965 showed that 75 percent favored federal voting rights legislation. [26] Seventy-five percent is a tremendous amount of favorability. However, the real question is, How adamant were those that did not support the legislation? If these voters were adamant enough, these laws just might be the catalyst to break off from a particular party.

Case in point, another Gallup poll in 1965 showed that 42 percent of the population indicated that the government was moving too fast in implementing voting rights legislation. [27] Although the implications of this 1965 Gallup poll was fascinating, the polling preceding the 1968 Fair Housing Act was much more revealing. In 1967, a Gallup poll declared that between 1963 and 1965, 69 to 71 percent of *whites* said they might move or would move if a great number of *negroes* moved into the neighborhood. [28] Shortly after the data were collected for that poll, the Fair Housing Act was passed.

Now the purpose of the last few pages is not to provide a mini lesson in civil rights or racial tensions of the sixties. The purpose is to set the tone for the conditions of that time. It is becoming clear that after two prior seminal civil rights acts, the 1968 Fair Housing Act, was to be the well-known *last straw* for a certain segment of the population. Furthermore, as a direct beneficiary, George Wallace garnered the support of millions of voters who were disgruntled with the direction of the country regarding civil rights policies (in addition to the other polarizing issues of that time). More importantly, regardless of the fact that several members of Republican members of congress voted for the Civil Rights Acts, these policies were perceived by the general population to be championed by the Democratic president at that time and thus the party.

---

[26] Isserman, Maurice & Kazin, Michael. *America Divided*, pg. 142

[27] Gallup, George & Gallup Jr., Alec. *The Gallup Poll 1999*, 2000, pg. 237

[28] Christopher Bonastia, *Knocking on the Door: The Federal Government's Attempt to Desegregate*, pg. 88, Princeton University Press, 2006

Once I realized that Wallace obtained a substantial amount of voters, who were mostly former Democrats disillusioned with the path that the country was moving in, it became apparent that civil rights legislation is most likely the primary catalyst that fractured the electorate. Although, there are additional reasons for the Wallace voters to break-off, race or civil rights was in the forefront in the 1968 election.[29]

To attempt to corroborate this claim, the 1968 election is added to the previous trend graph. The popular vote for 1968 election along with the popular vote for the presidential elections from 1972 through 2000 are compared (see Fig. 1-14).

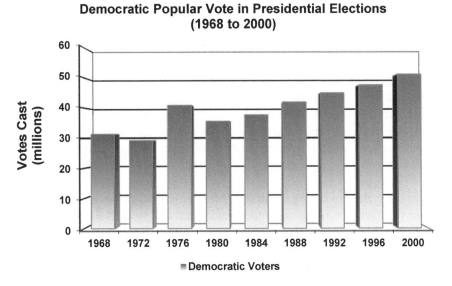

Democratic Popular Vote in Presidential Elections (1968 to 2000)

Source: US Census Bureau Statistical Abstracts 1942 to 2001 and uselectionatlas.org

Figure 1-14 1968 to 2000 Democratic Popular Vote

It is obvious that the 1968 Democratic popular vote had approximately the same amount as the 1972 election. Returning to the original theory, the hypothesis is that the fracturing of our electorate occurred in 1968 by many of the Wallace voters *splitting off* and deciding not to vote for the

---

[29] Lewis Gould, 1968: The Election that Changed America (Chicago: Ivan R. Dee, Inc., 1993)

Democratic candidate for president. When this fracturing occurred, it left essentially only the staunch core Democratic voters voting for the Democratic candidate.

Nonetheless, Senator Hubert Humphrey, the Democratic candidate in 1968, garnered more votes than Senator George McGovern did in 1972. This led to the conclusion that the fracturing occurred but was not complete in 1968. In 1968, a small amount of Humphrey's voters did *not* break off and instead continued to vote for the Democratic candidate. However, in the election of 1972, these voters ultimately dropped off, leaving an even smaller core group of Democratic voters. These voters in 1972 became the initial starting point for the Democratic electorate and the beginning of the presidential trend.

Summary Thoughts on the Trend

Although seeming unconventional, the theory of the presidential trend is fairly simple and straightforward. To summarize the theory, the polarizing issues of the turbulent sixties established the conditions whereby a significant catalyst, such as the series of civil rights laws occurring in a relatively short span of time, could theoretically splinter the country's electorate in two.

In reality, the fracturing consisted of a group of voters shifting *away* from the Democratic presidential candidates and toward the Republican or Independent candidates or simply not voting. This shifting produced two theoretical electorates: the Democratic and the non-Democratic electorates. The Democratic and non-Democratic electorates provide one of the keys to analyzing voting behavior at the presidential level. Instead of analyzing elections only in terms of Democrat, Republican and Independent, additional insight can be gleaned from dividing the analysis into *Democrat and non-Democrat*.

To continue, the shifting left mostly core Democratic voters voting for one type of candidate, the Democratic candidate. This isolation of the core Democratic candidate's voters plus a steady growth of new voters and a relatively constant number of swing voters led to the popular vote progressing in a *linear* manner for the Democratic candidates.

Thus, the *fracturing* of the electorate is actually a shifting of a portion of the electorate to another portion of the electorate. The fracturing theory works due to the existence of two core groups of voters that tend to only vote for a particular type of candidate. The Democratic electorate is isolated with mostly core Democratic voters. The other non-Democratic electorate contains mostly core Republican voters, in addition to the new group, of these shifting Independent or rather non-Democratic voters.

Besides the linear manner of the Democratic vote, further proof of the fracturing exists in the non-Democratic side. Since there are two types of candidates contained in the non-Democratic electorate (Republican and Independent), instead of three, the voting pattern of the two show a unique mirroring of each other. This distinctive mirroring only exists when there are two dominating candidates pulling voters away from each other.

It is important to reiterate that this fracturing might not have occurred and remained in effect, if it were not for the ongoing contentious issues percolating in the country. In other words, the original issues that existed in the sixties were not necessarily the issues that kept the presidential electorate split for almost 30 years. The new *wedge issues* of the seventies, eighties, and nineties—such as abortion, gay rights, and gun control—most likely became supplemental or in some cases replacement issues to voters who kept the two electorates separated for nearly three decades.

In addition to the new wedge issues, the original 1968 group that split-off and voted for the Independent candidate, as well as their voting offspring,[30] most likely became part of the Independent voters in 1992. Along the way, some of these voters merged into the Republican Party, but others in all probability continued to be non-Democrats and could possibly exist in today's current electorate (e.g. Tea Party voters). Nonetheless, regardless of the past or current makeup of the voters or the issues that continue to divide the electorate, the presidential trend remains a unique anomaly in US voting history and probably the *mother of all political realignments*.

---

[30] My terminology for descendants of voters whose voting behavior is passed down from generation to generation through "family socialization."

A Summary of the Presidential Trend

Chapter 2

Prelude to a Trend

Introduction

The previous chapter presents a concise summary of the entire presidential trend phenomenon. This chapter discusses the lead up to the fracturing of the electorate as well as an extension of the theory that proposes that the fracturing actually began with an earlier election. That particular election possesses a similar theme: a civil rights policy and a major third-party candidate that pulled voters away from the Democratic candidate.

The First Crack in the Electorate

The election of 1968 proved to be a critical election for the office of president. Our entire electorate almost divided itself into two parts. However, did the electorate fracture for the first time in 1968? Is there a previous election that had similar conditions and was a precursor for the actual fracturing that occurred in 1968?

Considering these questions, we should begin with an election that occurred prior to the 1968 election. The year was 1948. The president was Harry S. Truman. The upcoming election that year would prove to be foreshadowing for the critical election that would come twenty years later.

With a distinct similarity to 1968, in 1948, President Truman issued two executive orders that were controversial for that time: 1) banning segregation in the armed forces (Executive Order 9981); and 2) guaranteeing of fair employment practices in the civil service (Executive

Order 9980). [31] Though these initiatives may not be controversial by today's standards, they were extremely controversial in the 1940s. Prior to these initiatives, Truman established the President's Committee on Civil Rights and became the first president to address the National Association for the Advancement of Colored People (NAACP). [32] This speech made Truman the first president to commit himself and the federal government to civil rights and human freedom of black Americans. [33]

As a side note, another foreshadowing event occurred in 1948 when an organization known as the Americans for Democratic Action (A.D.A.) drafted a minority report. The report included an amendment that commended Truman for "his courageous stand on the issue of civil rights." A.D.A.'s spokesman at that time was Hubert Horatio Humphrey Jr., the mayor of Minneapolis, Minnesota. Hubert Humphrey would end up playing a role in the next phase of the creation of the trend 20 years later. [34]

Running in the upcoming presidential election of 1948 against Truman was the Republican, Thomas E. Dewey. Also running in the 1948 election was a relatively young governor, James "Strom" Thurman of South Carolina. Thurman, who was a Democrat at the time, ran for president under a new third party called the States' Rights or Dixiecrat" Party. The Dixiecrats, which consisted mostly of individuals who splintered off from the Democratic Party because of the support that the party had for several controversial civil rights planks.

In the 1948 election, Thurman received over a million votes and a little over 2 percent (2.4 percent) of the popular vote. Although Thurman received a relatively small percentage of the popular vote, he carried four southern states: Alabama, Louisiana, Mississippi, and of course his home state of South Carolina (see Fig. 2-1). To illustrate how unusual this was, since that time there has been only one other non-majority party candidate for president to win a state. Nevertheless, as a result of

---

[31] Michael R. Gardner, *Harry Truman and Civil Rights: Moral Courage and Political Risks*, Southern Illinois University Press 2002
[32] ibid
[33] ibid
[34] ibid

Thurman's failed bid for the presidency, the Dixiecrat Party quickly dissolved after the election. Consequently, the old Dixiecrat voters would ultimately return and vote for the Democratic candidate in future elections. Still, the 1948 election produced the first *fissure* in the voting electorate.[35] The voters in this election were disenchanted and shifted away from the Democratic candidates during that year. However, this breaking away was only temporary, and they later came back to vote for Democratic candidates in the years leading up to the 1968 and 1972 elections where they ultimately *split off*. Chapter 6 reviews an element of the trend theory that brings to life the critical nature of the 1948 election and perhaps the impetus for the current *core* group of voters.

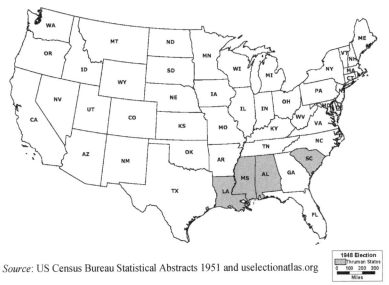

Source: US Census Bureau Statistical Abstracts 1951 and uselectionatlas.org

Figure 2-1 States Won by Strom Thurman in the 1948 Election

Even though Thurman's run for the presidency was fairly unsuccessful, it foreshadowed what was yet to come in 1968[36]—that is to say, embittered Democrats and a substantial splintering off from the Democratic Electorate.

---

[35] For the purpose of this book, the voting electorate refers to voters who vote for the office of president.
[36] Thurman later switched his party from Democrat to Republican in 1964.

The Turbulent '60s

After the 1940s, the 1950s carried with it some major civil rights occurrences for the country including Brown v. Board of Education, the Montgomery Bus Boycott, and the desegregation of Little Rock High School. Although these events represented major strides in the country's movement toward expanding civil rights, no particular political party could be credited or, as opponents would say, "blamed," for these advancements. Although, the fifties included no major *legislative* changes, that was not the case for the sixties. In addition, the legislative changes of the sixties carried with them a political party to blame.

The 1960s were certainly ripe for some type of dramatic political occurrence. In fact, as previously noted, some have labeled this period, "The Turbulent '60s."[37] For example, during the 1960s there were several notable assassinations, including Medgar Evers, John F. Kennedy, Malcolm X, Martin Luther King Jr., and Robert F. Kennedy. In addition, the Cold War heated up; a sexual revolution began; recreational use of drugs was thriving; and last but certainly not least, the war in Vietnam was causing unrest in the country.

Each of these major issues of the sixties carried social, cultural, and, more importantly, political implications. Furthermore, the political dimensions were polarizing. That is to say, the political gap between those who considered themselves liberal (associated with the Democrats) and those who considered themselves conservative (associated with the Republicans) was widening. In other words, the issues of the sixties were pulling voters away from each other and thus our voting electorate apart. Consequently, this increase in political distinctions, in addition to the critical differences on civil rights, set the stage for an extremely polarized electorate and the *mother of all electoral realignments.*

---

[37] Greenhaven Press's 10 book series, *The Turbulent '60s* explores this remarkable decade.

The 1968 Election

The conflict during the early sixties was simply setting the stage for the election of 1968. Twenty years after Strom Thurman's bid for the presidency in 1948, the fracturing that almost occurred completed its course. Although the years had changed, the critical issue remained the same: civil rights. The year was 1968. The president this time was Lyndon Baines Johnson. The disgruntled ex-Democratic candidate this time was Governor George Corley Wallace of Alabama.

As with Strom Thurman, Wallace ran for president under a new third party called the American Independent Party. Also like Thurman, Wallace *was* a Democrat. Finally, yet importantly, similar to Thurman's Party, an underlying theme of the American Independent Party was the opposition to a series of civil rights laws. Specifically, this included the 1964 Civil Rights Act, 1965 Voting Rights Act and, more importantly, the 1968 Civil Rights Act otherwise known as the Fair Housing Act. The importance of the 1968 Fair Housing Act is that it prohibited discrimination in the sale, rental, and financing of housing. In essence, the act gave African Americans the right to purchase or rent homes located in predominantly white neighborhoods. For some whites, this proverbial *last straw* broke the camel's back—or, in this case, the last straw that split the electorate apart.

Even though Wallace attempted to shift the focus of the American Independent Party platform to communism and blue-collar issues, "States' Rights" remained an umbrella issue during the campaign of 1968. States' rights at that time was *code* for the federal government no longer interfering with the rights of a state to enact or modify its own civil rights laws. Of course, pushing for states' rights was done to appeal to many white voters in the southern states.

Nevertheless, unlike Thurman, George Wallace received over 9.9 million votes and over 13.5 percent of the popular vote.[38] Consequently, Wallace obtained the largest popular vote at the time for a third party candidate since 1924[39] (see Fig. 2-2).

---

[38] US Census Bureau, *Statistical Abstract of the United States*, 2001
[39] In 1924 Robert LaFollette of the Independent Progressive candidate received 17 percent of the popular vote.

In order to fully understand the tenor of Wallace's campaign of 1968, it is first useful to recall his gubernatorial election in Alabama that occurred only a few years earlier in 1962. Wallace was elected governor of Alabama on a pro-segregation, pro-states' rights platform. In his infamous inaugural speech, he stated, "Segregation now, segregation tomorrow, and segregation forever." In addition, in June of 1963, he stood in front of a schoolhouse door at the University of Alabama in an attempt to stop the desegregation of that institution by the enrollment of two African-American students.[40]

Later in 1964, using his recognized public image created by the University of Alabama controversy, Wallace ran, albeit unsuccessfully, for the Democratic nomination for president. Wallace remaining in the Democratic Party and seeking the nomination is an important factor in unraveling the origin of the trend. Because Wallace ran for the nomination of Democratic Party, he was essentially condoning working within the system of the Democratic Party. Consequently, there was no splintering of the Democratic Electorate and President Lyndon Johnson, a Democrat, cruised to an easy victory (see Fig. 2-2).

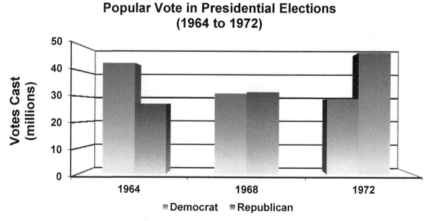

Source: US Census Bureau Statistical Abstract of the US, 2004 (Table HS-52)

Figure 2-2 Popular Vote in Presidential Elections
(1964 to 1972)

---

[40] Vivian Malone and James Hood were blocked from entering the University of Alabama in 1963.

Nevertheless, in 1968, Wallace abandoned the Democratic Party to help expand the American Independent Party. Similar to Strom Thurman in 1948, Wallace carried five southern states: Alabama, Arkansas, Georgia, Louisiana, and Mississippi (see Fig. 2-3). Since Wallace was no longer working within the framework of the Democratic Party, his candidacy would prove devastating to the Democrats. Essentially, his former Democratic voters left the party along with him.

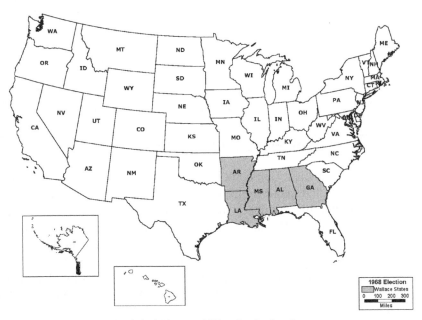

Sources: US Census Bureau Statistical Abstracts 1970 and uselectionatlas.org

Figure 2-3 States Won by Wallace in the 1968 Election

During the same time that Wallace was adamantly against the newly enacted federal civil rights and voting rights laws, Richard Milhous Nixon, the Republican, began deploying the "Southern Strategy."[41] The Southern Strategy was aligned almost perfectly with George Wallace's position in that it promoted states' rights in order to appeal to many southern white voters.

---

[41] The Southern Strategy enabled Richard Nixon to compete and win in the Democrat-dominated south.

Thus the voters had a choice: Democrats opposing states' rights while Republicans and American Independent Party's supporting them. The southern voters did make a choice. The Republican candidate, Richard Nixon, carried three Deep South[42] states while Wallace carried five. The Democratic candidate, Hubert Humphrey, ultimately carried no Deep South states.

The popular vote for Humphrey[43], totaled over 31.3 million while the votes cast for Nixon, was only slightly higher at 31.9 million (see Table 2-1). The electoral outcome that Wallace ultimately garnered was over 9.9 million votes. This is certainly a significant amount.

Table 2-1 Popular Vote in Pres. Elections, 1964 to 1972 (millions)

	1964	1968	1972
Democrat	43.1	31.3	29.2
Republican	27.2	31.8	47.2
Other	.03	10.2	1.4

Source: US Census Bureau Statistical Abstract of the United States, 2004

Since Wallace ran as a Democrat in the prior presidential election (1964) and had a base that came from the Democratic south[44], arguably a case can be made that his candidacy in 1968 shifted enough votes away from Humphrey to allow Nixon to win the popular vote. [45] Not only did Wallace possibly shift votes away from Humphrey in 1968, his candidacy corresponded with a realignment that would exist for at least the next three decades. In essence, those voters who voted for Wallace in 1968 did not return back to vote for the Democratic candidate for president—with one exception, 1976.

---

[42] Deep South states are defined as Alabama, Arkansas, Georgia, Florida, Mississippi and Louisiana, South Carolina, and Tennessee.

[43] Coincidentally, Hubert Humphrey was one of the central members of Congress who lead the push for civil rights when Strom Thurman ran for president in 1948.

[44] Even though his base was in the South, Wallace obtained votes from just about all parts of the country.

[45] See www.presidentelect.org/art_sheppard_e2000an.html

Chapter 3

The Realignment

Introduction

Because of the increasing polarization of the 1960s, stress had been building in the US population and, unbeknownst to the average citizen, the voting electorate as well. Ultimately, this stress, in addition to the support that certain Democratic leaders placed on passing civil rights laws, was strong enough to cause a major political realignment that resulted in the creation of a new fractured electorate. This political realignment was predicted by President Lyndon Johnson when he made his legendary statement of: "I think we have just delivered the South to the Republican Party for a long time to come."[46]

Past Realignments or Trends

Political analysts have studied and uncovered major electoral realignments for decades. Many political analysts developed realignment theories during the 1900s. V.O. Key stands out as one of the dominant theorist. His 1955 article, *A Theory of Critical Elections*, stated that parties in American elections routinely shift dramatically back and forth. However, prior to Key's seminal article was Louis H. Bean who was not always credited with contributing substantially to political theory. Ironically, the 1948 presidential election played a vital role in Bean's prominence.[47] He leaped into celebrated distinction when he predicted

---

[46] *New York Times, Divisive Words: News Analysis; GOP'S 40 Years of Juggling on Race* 2002, Adam Clymer.
[47] Also ironic, Bean had deep concerns about the splintered "Dixiecrat" party stripping votes away from Truman.

that in 1948 Harry Truman, the Democratic president at the time, would beat Thomas Dewey, the Republican challenger. At that time, all other major analysts predicted a win for Dewey. One of the most famous pictures of that era is of Truman holding up a *Chicago Daily Tribune* newspaper with a headline that reads: "Dewey Defeats Truman." Bean of course was correct, and the newspaper was wrong. For that prognostication, in 1951, the magazine *Business Week* called him "The Best-Known Prophet Since Daniel."[48]

One of the fundamental concepts of Bean's as well as other's forecasting centered on "political cycles," or as he called them "political tides." These cycles or tides reoccur and last for approximately two or three decades. Like tidal waves, the political dominance flows in, giving rise to a new party control.

Yet what occurred in 1968 was not a simple political tidal-wave change. It was another type of natural phenomenon, something akin to an earthquake. The stress that had been building on the voting electorate, due to the growing polarizing issues and pressures of the sixties to adopt and implement civil rights laws, had gotten to the breaking point. Like stress that is placed on tectonic plates in the earth, the pressure builds to a certain point and then fracturing occurs—in other words, an earthquake. In this case, the earthquake was a major fracturing or realignment of the voting electorate.[49] Some earthquakes fracture and leave a gaping *crack* between landmasses. Such was the case for our presidential electorate. In the 1968 electoral earthquake, there was a separation with two fractured pieces of the electorate that never came back together (excluding a small portion). In essence, once the total voting electorate separated, two distinct electorates were created.[50] More importantly, each of these new voting electorates contained voters who rarely crossed over to the other electorate.

The fragmentation and isolation of voters from the other part of the electorate was the crux of the predictable trend. Here lies the first key to unraveling the trend's mystery. Once a sizable number of voters were removed, the Democratic Electorate was left with a smaller and more

---

[48] *Business Week*, August 18, 1951 pg. 66.
[49] Political Scientist V.O. Key called these realignments "critical" elections
[50] See Chapter 4.

consistent group of voters. In essence, the Democratic Electorate had now become mostly loyal voters (see Chap. 6). Consequently, those remaining individuals were extremely reliable when it came to voting for the Democratic candidate for president. An important note is that this phenomenon seems to have occurred at the presidential level.[51] Those individuals who splintered off continued to vote for different parties at the state and local level for years to come.[52] Nonetheless, the same voters, in addition to a proportional amount of newly registered voters continue to vote for the Democratic candidate.

On the other hand, not all of those voters who separated from the Democratic electorate in 1968 became Republicans. Many were and still are purely non-Democratic voters (see Chap. 13). Here lies another important deduction. Non-Democratic voters will mostly vote for the Republican or Independent candidate or will *not* vote.

A Predictable Trend

There was no indication of a consistent predictable trend in the popular vote for the Democratic candidate from 1948 to 1968 (see Fig. 3-1).

After the election of 1968, the fragmentation of the Democratic Electorate continued to erode slightly until the 1972 election. Essentially, the voting electorate for the Democratic candidate for president *bottoms* out in 1972[53] (see also Fig. 3-1).

From this point on, with the exception of the 1976 election, the popular vote for the Democratic candidate would always increase in a consistent fashion. In other words, votes cast would follow a predictable trend, from election to election (see Fig. 3-2).

---

[51] It is important to note that this phenomenon exists at the presidential level and not necessarily at the state or lower levels.

[52] Democrats continue to win at US Senate and House elections and lower levels until the 1990s.

[53] This *bottoming out* most likely was due to the election of 1968, including some *holdouts* of the non-Democrats that would ultimately split off from the Democratic Party in 1972.

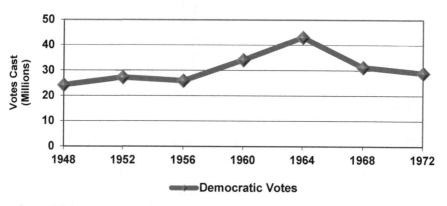

Source: US Census Bureau Statistical Abstracts 2004

Figure 3-1 Democratic Popular Vote
(1948 to 1972)

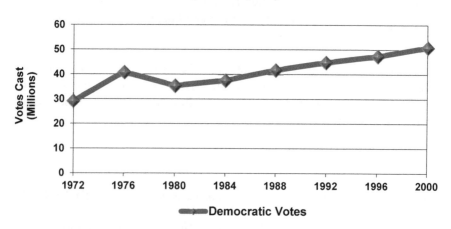

Source: US Census Bureau Statistical Abstracts 2004

Figure 3-2 Democratic Popular Vote
(1972 to 2000)

Once the assumption is made that votes cast for the Democratic candidate consisted of only steadfast reliable Democratic voters, who essentially always voted, it is easy to see how the popular vote becomes predictable. In essence, the vote for the Democratic candidate from 1972 to 2000 (excluding 1976), for the most part, did not consist of Independent or Republican voters that may vote for the Democrat. It did not consist of voters who swing back and forth between voting for Democratic candidates and candidates of other parties. It only consisted of voters who always vote for the Democratic candidate. On the other hand, the Republican candidate's votes consist of core Republican voters in addition to voters who swung between non-majority party candidates and simply not voting (see Fig. 3-3).

It is important to stress the point that this did not mean that the Democratic candidate receives absolutely *no* votes from the non-majority party or Republican voters. It simply meant that those types of voters made up such a small portion of the popular vote for the Democratic candidate. Likewise, a very small percentage of Democratic voters may have voted for Republican or Independent candidates.

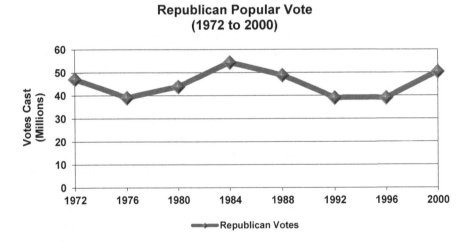

Source: US Census Bureau Statistical Abstracts 2004

Figure 3-3 Republican Popular Vote
(1972 to 2000)

In addition, there were most likely voters who, when asked (i.e., polled), would self-identify themselves as Independent voters but consistently vote for the Democratic candidate for president.[54] The end result is that when those individuals voted in presidential elections they voted only for or mostly for the Democratic candidate. Thus when polled they may have responded that they were independent; however, they remained part of the Democratic Electorate in presidential elections. A better method of viewing the partisan nature of these voters is to analyze the previous vote for these voters. Chap. 13 presents exit poll data and compares it with the trend.

Sustaining the Fractured Electorate

In order for the presidential trend to be sustained for over 30 years, the fracturing of the voting electorate must have been maintained. The very existence of the trend relies on the continued separation of the two electorates: Democrat and non-Democrat. If the two electorates ever merge back together, the Democratic linear trend and mirror effect would vanish. Thus how did the voting electorate continue to be divided? The answer lies with something that most of us are exposed to from the day we are born.

Since the pressures of the events of the 1960s seems to be the impetus for the fracturing of the voting electorate, at first glance it could be assumed that those factors continue to be the central reason. This is most likely *not* the case.

First, voters who were old enough to vote in 1968 may have been part of the fracturing of the electorate because of certain issues at the time. It is important to note that the same issues that existed to cause the fracturing may not be the same issues that kept or keep the two electorates apart. For example, the 1960s' issues such as the sexual revolution, recreational drug use, female liberation, and of course civil rights were the catalysts for the fracturing of the electorate. However, in the 1970s additional *wedge* issues such as the war in Vietnam (now a Republican issue), affirmative action, and abortion became seminal issues that continued the

---

[54] This would result in tracking or exit polls showing a higher percentage of Independent voters voting for the Democratic candidate. A similar situation most likely occurs with Republican voters.

division. The 1980s saw the addition of gun control, and in the 1990s gay rights came in to play to continue the separation between the Democrat and non-Democratic Electorate for the next couple of decades.

Second, what continued the separation with new registered voters was due to *family socialization*. Family socialization is the process whereby the youth learn the rules, traditions, and acceptable interactions of a particular society. When it comes to politics, some analysts suggest that major party affiliation is also passed down from generation to generation.[55] This most likely is the primary element for the perpetuation of core or base voters for each major party. Therefore, Democrats spawn Democratic children and Republican spawn Republican children, etc.

I ultimately conclude that for over 30 years, the Democrat and non-Democratic Electorates remained separate because of old and new issues that divided our country. Thus, the electorates have remained divided as they increased in population due mostly to family socialization.

The Exception to the Rule: 1976?

Undoubtedly one of the fundamental questions by now is what happened in 1976? The political answer is that the election of 1976 is a prime example of a *deviating election*.[56] From a statistical point of view, this would often be called an outlier. Nonetheless, a deviating election is an election that, because of certain unique circumstances, does not conform to the normal political trend or cycle.

Specifically, 1976 may have been an exception because of a major event or major events that occurred prior to the election. Therefore, some unique event, instance, or occurrence needed to be found to make it an exception. What occurred around or prior to the 1976 election that is exceptional?

In the 1976 election, the sitting president was Republican Gerald Ford and his Democratic opposition was Georgia Governor Jimmy Carter.

---

[55] Angus Campbell, Warren E. Miller, Philip E. Converse, and Donald E. Stokes, *The American Voter*, 1960

[56] A deviating election is an election whereby the party out of power wins the election.

Carter being a southern governor boded well for him in the election that year. In fact, in 1976 he carried every Southern state except for Virginia. [57] However, one additional element contributed to the performance of Jimmy Carter that year: Watergate.

To provide a refresher, Watergate is the name coined for the scandal involving Republican President Richard Nixon. The scandal began with five men being arrested after breaking and entering into the headquarters of the Democratic National Committee (DNC) at the Watergate Hotel complex in Washington, DC. It ended with a cover-up of the break-in. President Nixon and his staff's problem was not the break-in itself, but that they conspired to cover up the activities of the break-in.

Because of the scandal, Congress initiated the process for the impeachment of Nixon. Ultimately, President Nixon resigned before the impeachment process could be completed. Nonetheless, Richard Nixon's resignation is the first and only resignation of a president in United States' history. Gerald Ford, who was Nixon's vice president, assumed the presidency in August of 1976. He was, inexplicably, linked to Nixon and thus to Watergate. Consequently, Watergate, an unusual and dramatic milestone for the presidency, caused the anomaly or the *exception to the rule* for the presidential trend theory. In effect, those voters who fractured off from the Democratic Party in 1968 and 1972 decided to come back for one election and vote for Jimmy Carter.

However, this election anomaly adds a footnote to the Carter presidency that may go a small way toward rebuilding his presidential legacy. Because of his loss in 1980 and the economic conditions that arose during his presidency, Jimmy Carter has been maligned by many political pundits and analysts. That being said, regardless of whether or not the central cause of his winning in 1976 was due to Watergate, President Carter attracted significant non-Democratic voters and should go down in history as the only Democratic presidential candidate to *break away* from the presidential trend and exceed its limitations (see Fig. 3-4).

---

[57] Robert P. Steed, Laurence W. Moreland, Tod A. Baker, *Southern Parties and Elections: Studies in Regional Political Change*, 2012

Thus, the ironic revealing of the trend is that Jimmy Carter's voter performance in 1976 is better than any other Democratic presidential candidate during the trend period. However, in retrospect, Carter could do practically nothing to win once the deviating election was over. By 1980, Democratic voters fell back in line with the presidential trend that began in 1972 (see Fig. 3-4).

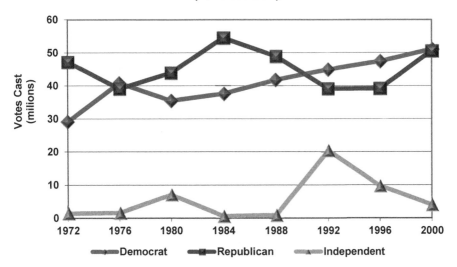

Democratic, Republican & Independent Popular Vote (1972 to 2000)

Sources: US Census Bureau Statistical Abstracts 2004 and uselectionatlas.org

Figure 3-4 Democratic, Republican & Independent Popular Vote (1972 to 2000)

The Realignment

Chapter 4

The New Electorate and Non-Democrats

Introduction

One of the realities of the trend is that, after the major realignment in 1968, the voting electorate at the presidential level was fractured into two main groups: Democrats and non-Democrats (see Fig. 4-1). The simple duality of voters was caused by the pressures applied to the electorate contributing to a sizable amount of voters splintering off (see Chap. 2). This essentially left the voting electorate divided into two main groups[58]: a Democratic Electorate and non-Democratic Electorate[59]. These two groups, especially the non-Democratic voters, made a conscience decision to *not* vote for the candidates of the other group or as W.C. Fields put it, "I never vote for anyone. I always vote against."

A New Voting Electorate

When the electorate fractured, it cracked, leaving mostly *core* voters remaining in the Democratic electorate. These voters always or mostly voted for the Democratic candidate in presidential elections. Furthermore, these voters also seemed to turn out to vote in most presidential elections. [60] On the other hand, those who were part of the non-Democratic electorate, rarely or never voted for the Democratic

---

[58] Many Democrats may classify themselves as Independents but vote for the Democratic candidate most of the time. Also, a small portion of the voting electorate continues to sway between the Democrat and non-Democrat electorates.

[59] For the purpose of this book, these two electorates do not consist of voters who are eligible but do not vote.

[60] The reason why Democratic voters seem to always vote may be due to its ongoing critical get out the vote (GOTV) efforts.

candidate, but instead voted for the Republican or the Independent candidates[61], or they simply did not vote at all (see Table 4-1). As Table 4-1 indicates, the Democratic candidate obtained votes primarily from voters who voted solely for Democratic candidates (with a consistent group of swing voters). The non-Democratic candidates garnered votes mostly from four (4) different groups: voters who voted Republican; voters who voted for Independent candidates; voters who voted for both Republican and Independent candidates; and voters who sometimes did not vote.

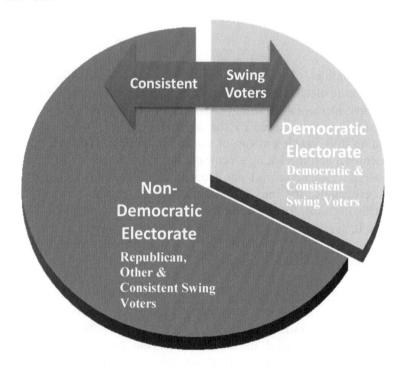

Figure 4-1 Voting Electorate in Presidential
Elections After 1968

---

[61] Other candidates include Independent, Green, Reform, and other third-party candidates.

Table 4-1 Voting Electorate After 1968	
Democratic Electorate	**Non-Democratic Electorate**
Voters who vote for Democratic candidates	Voters who vote Republican candidates
Consistent swing of Rep./Independent Voters	Voters who vote for Independent candidates
	Voters who vote for Republican and Independent candidates
	Voters who sometimes do not vote
	Consistent swing of Dem. Voters

It was expected that the popular vote would have increased as the voting age population increases. However, the caveat was that it *only* showed the increase in voting age population and ultimately those who turned out to vote. The emphasis is on the *only*. This means that just about every other factor had *not* noticeably influenced the vote for the Democratic candidate—except the increase in population. This included factors such as different election turnout percentages, candidates, and current domestic or global conditions. Just about any other aspect that you can think of did *not* have an impact on the votes cast for the Democratic candidate (other than the growth in voting age population).[62] A review of the consistency of the Democratic votes cast was demonstrated by analyzing the turnout percentage of the Democratic popular vote and the Republican popular vote. When compared with the overall voting age population (VAP) from 1972 to 2000 (excluding 1976), the ratio of the Democratic popular vote to VAP varied from only 21.4 percent to 25.2 percent (3.8 percent) while the Republican popular vote to VAP varied from 20.2 to 34.6 percent (14.4 percent).

It is important to note that just as the total voting age population of the United States consisted of those persons who immigrated to this country as well as those that left the country (emigrants), such is the case for those who vote for the Democratic candidate. The popular vote for the Democratic candidate consisted of three different types of voters:

1) Persons who voted for the Democratic candidate in the previous election; plus

---

[62] I later discovered that the trend associated with the total voting age population is less even linear than the Democratic trend.

2) Persons who previously voted for the Republican or Independent Party's candidates in the previous election; plus

3) Persons who were first-time voters or did not vote in the previous election.

Voters who swung back and forth (Republican/Independent voters to Democratic voters and back) could not be of a substantial amount and must have been consistent from election to election (see Chap. 13). Just as estimates of voting age population included a level of immigration and emigration and still possessed a linear trend, the presidential trend also included some level of outflow/inflow, but not enough to deter its linear status. Although the outflow and inflow of persons tend to cancel each other out, the significant population was persons who voted for the Democratic candidate for president in previous elections.

Also, most of the increase from year to year in the voting age population trend was attributed to the increase obtained from new voters who just turned 18 years of age. Likewise, the increase from election year to year of the presidential trend was attributed to new voters added to existing voters.

The core of this theory should be confirmable. If the popular vote for the Democratic candidate is made up of mostly first-time voters plus the popular vote of the Democratic candidate in the previous election, there should be a way to verify this. Since data for the popular vote are already acquired, there is only the need for data on first-time voters.

Since data from this source was available from 1984, this became the starting point for the analysis. [63] Using the total popular vote, percentage of first-time voters, and partisan portion of those voters, the number of first-time voters for each party designation was estimated. From the popular vote plus an estimated number of first-time voters, a projected amount for the popular vote is calculated and an accuracy-derived. [64]

---

[63] The *New York Times* gathered data from Edison Media Research/Mitofsky International, Voter Research and Survey and the Voter News Services located at http://elections.nytimes.com/2008/results/president/exit-polls.html.

[64] The 1980 popular vote of 35.5 million was used for the estimate of 1984.

Thus, a simple formula is used to calculate the popular vote for the Democratic candidate in a given election year. It is

$$(PVD_{Current}) = (PVD_{Previous}) + (FVD_{Current}),$$

where $PVD_{Current}$ is the popular vote for the Democratic candidate for a given presidential year, $PVD_{Previous}$ is the popular vote for the Democratic candidate for the previous presidential year, and $FVD_{Current}$ is first-time new voters plus voters who did not vote in the previous election.

As Table 4-2 indicates, the accuracy of adding the number of first-time voters plus the previous popular vote for the Democratic candidates is no less than 95.4 percent with an average of 97.5 percent. If the same type of formula and accuracy check is determined for the Republican candidates, the accuracy is as low as 69.9 percent with an average of 83.5 percent.

Table 4-2 Estimate of First-time Voters & Accuracy of Popular Vote Estimate, 1984 to 2000

	1984	1988	1992	1996	2000
First-Time Democratic Voters (Mil)	2.8	3.0	2.9	4.7	4.9
First-Time Republican Voters (Mil)	4.5	3.3	2.0	2.9	4.1
First-Time Independents Voters (Mil)			1.4	1.0	0.4
Total Democratic Voters Actual (Mil)	37.6	41.8	44.9	47.4	51.0
Total Democratic Voters est. (Mil)	38.3	40.6	44.7	49.6	52.3
Accuracy of Democratic est., %	98.1	97.1	99.5	95.4	97.4
Total Republican Voters Actual (Mil)	54.5	48.9	39.1	39.2	50.5
Total Republican Voters est. (Mil)	48.4	57.7	50.9	42.1	43.3
Accuracy of Republican est., %	88.9	81.9	69.9	92.7	85.8

Sources: *New York Times* exit polls; US Census Bureau Statistical Abstracts 2001

The stunning accuracy of the projections for the Democratic popular vote using the previous election plus the first-time voters is another clear piece of evidence that the trend exists. Visual substantiation can be seen by viewing the graph in Fig. 4.2.

Although the graph clearly shows a higher accuracy rate for the projected amount of Democratic votes, it is important to remember one vital stipulation. These voters, who formed the presidential trend, did so in *presidential elections.* Elections at other levels (congressional, gubernatorial, etc.) may not have displayed aspects of the trend.[65] In other words, these unique voters form a trend when voting in presidential elections.

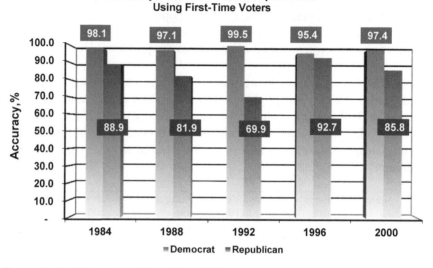

Source: *New York Times* exit poll data 1984 to 2000

Figure 4-2 Accuracy of Estimated Popular Vote Using First-time Voters (1984 to 2000)

The fact that this trend only shows up at the presidential level could be one of the reasons why it has not been discovered and written about thus far. Some analysts tend to describe and lump voters together despite the type of elections (e.g., a Democratic voter in presidential elections is a Democratic voter in congressional elections). Some voters may most likely vote differently depending upon the office level.

Nonetheless, the theory of the previous Democratic voters voting for the Democratic candidate plus essentially first-time votes seems to reflect

---

[65] I do believe that this trend, at the presidential level, is the preverbal *canary in the coal mine.* In other words, the effects of the trend will eventually manifest itself at lower office levels.

the same linearity as the actual popular vote. However, is there other evidence that the electorate had been fractured and the Democratic portion only or mostly included Democratic voters? This is investigated in the next section.

No Effect from the Non-Democratic Candidates

To recap, the central theory of this book is that the electorate had been fractured into two parts: one essentially included mostly Democratic voters while the other, the non-Democratic side, included Republican and other Independent voters (see Fig. 4-1). Consequently, if the electorate had truly been fractured, with the result being the *presidential trend*, what other evidence beside the trend could be visible because of this fracturing? Could there have been some other trend or trends created due to the fracturing? Each electorate needs to be considered separately and in order to discover additional proof that validates the fracturing electorate.

To verify the Democratic side, provided evidence shows that this electorate seems to contain only *one type of voter*. These were voters who essentially voted only for the Democratic candidates. In this theoretical electoral fracturing, the Democratic candidates were isolated from the voters for the Republican or other Independent candidates. Since there were only voters voting for the Democratic candidate in this portion of the electorate, there should have been some evidence of votes for the Democratic candidates *not* being affected by the votes for the Republican, Independent Party candidates or both. In theory, the two exist in two separate electorates.

This assumption relies on the fact that in normal elections, one candidate pulls or takes votes away from the other candidate. However, if you only have voters voting for a single candidate (or party), there should be no pulling of these votes away. This means there should be no decrease in the Democratic candidates' votes with an increase in votes for Republican or even Independent candidates.

Therefore, the votes cast for the Democratic candidates are viewed along with the votes for Republicans and then Independent candidates. If these votes cast were plotted on a line graph, there should have been a *dip* in the graph of one candidate's votes with the *increase* in the other. If this dip was apparent, it would have been an indication that there was a *pulling* away of votes from one candidate to another. If not, it would have been a clear indication of them being isolated from each other.

When the Democratic and Republican candidates votes are placed on a graph, the chart reveals that there are no noticeable effects of one candidates votes on another (see Fig. 4-3).

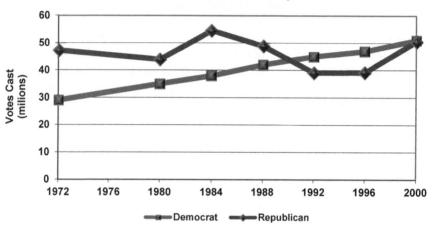

Democratic & Republican Popular Vote
(1972 to 2000 w/o 1976)

Sources: US Census Bureau Statistical Abstracts 1942 to 2001 and uselectionatlas.org

Figure 4-3 Democratic & Independent Popular Vote
(1972 to 2000, w/o 1976)

Under normal circumstances, votes cast for the Republican candidates should have had some effect on the Democratic candidates' votes or vice versa. Clearly, the graph shows none (or at best very little). Next, the Democratic and Independent party candidates' votes are plotted to determine if these two had any effect on one another. Again, since the theoretical Democratic electorate contained only voters voting for the Democratic candidate and the Independent Party candidates exist in a separate electorate, there should not have been any effect on one another.

As Fig. 4-4 shows, once again there is no noticeable effect. The most impressive aspects of the graph are the 1980, 1992, and 1996 elections. None of these votes cast for the non-majority party candidates had any effect on the Democratic candidates' votes. In spite of the extraordinarily high amount of votes received by the Independent candidates, the trend remains intact.

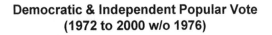

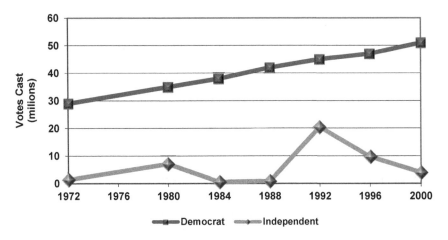

Sources: US Census Bureau Statistical Abstracts 1942 to 2001 and uselectionatlas.org

Figure 4-4 Democratic & Independent Popular Vote
(1972 to 2000, w/o 1976)

These two graphs validate the theory that the Democratic electorate only contained voters that vote for the Democratic candidates. Undoubtedly, these two charts show evidence of the Democratic Electorate being isolated from the Republican and Independent candidate's voters.

The graphs depict evidence that there is no indication that the number of votes received by the Republican or the Independent candidates did not have an impact on the votes for the Democratic candidate. The next step is to investigate the Non-Democratic electorate to obtained additional proof of the fracturing at the presidential level.

In addition to the linearity of the Democratic candidates' votes, there is a second and just as fascinating effect caused by the fracturing of the electorate. This occurred in the other electorate, the non-Democratic electorate. The effect reveals a relationship between the votes cast for the Republican candidate and the votes cast for the Independent candidates.

The Mirror Image Effect

In the theoretical other electorate, the non-Democratic side, there were essentially two types of voters. They included those who voted for the Republican candidates and those who voted for Independent candidates.

For the non-Democratic Electorate, a method is required to developed that would detect that only two types of candidates are contained in this second electorate. A voting pattern that reflected only two categories of candidates needs to be formulated. In other words, unlike the Democratic Electorate, the voting pattern should reflect only two types of candidates or parties directly *pulling* voters away from each other. It is important to reiterate that this analysis, as well as others in this book, relies on lumping all of the Independent candidates into one category.

The method developed, for the purpose of verifying that only two types of voters are contained in the electorate, is to detect a symmetrical inverse relationship or the previously noted "mirror effect." To illustrate the concept of the *ideal* mirror effect, a graph is created that depicts a simple two-party race (see Fig. 4-5).

The graph reveals a unique pattern, a mirroring of the two different party's votes. It is important to note that the voting pattern would be different if three different candidates or parties were battling for the same voters. In a scenario with three candidates, they each can take votes away from each other, not just from one single candidate. Hence, there likely should not be a distinctive mirror effect.

However, in a two-person race, especially ones where voters tend to turn out at the same rate, the graph results in a mirror image. In addition, not only is mirroring an important finding for this publication, but it could be used to show evidence or a fracturing in other types of elections as well.

Example of Ideal Mirroring of Votes Cast for Two Parties

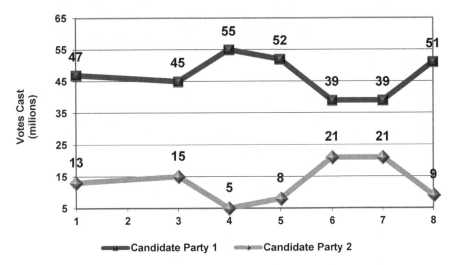

Figure 4-5 Example of Ideal Mirroring of Votes Cast for Two Parties

The mirror image exists due to the candidates vying for the same voters. In addition, the two combined make up the total votes counted. In the example, if all persons voted, and 60 voters turned out with one party receiving 47 votes, then the other party must have received 13 votes. If one party received 45 votes, then the other party must have received only 15 votes. Essentially, one party received a certain amount of votes while the other received the remaining amount. This example of ideal mirroring assumed 60 total voters for each election and, more importantly, every voter voted. If the turnout of total votes fluctuated, the ideal mirror pattern would not be produced. This of course is what occurs under realistic conditions. Therefore there should never be an exact mirror image under true electoral conditions.

In the theoretical non-Democratic electorate, voters essentially voted only for the Republican or Independent candidates (with Independent candidates grouped together). Thus, we had a similar situation as the above example. Specifically, we should have been able to identify the same effect as above, the mirror effect. The reason for this is simple. As Fig. 4-6 indicates, the non-Democratic candidates are fighting for the same voters.[66] Thus, if the Republican candidates performed well, they would have drawn voters away from the Independent candidates. Likewise, if the Independent candidates performed well, they would have drawn voters from the Republican candidates. Consequently, there should have been a decrease for one when there was an increase of the other and vice versa.

One last option is that a number of these non-Democrats may have chosen to not vote. As a result, neither the Republican nor the Independent candidates garnered these votes. The third option of not voting interjected an increased possibility of non-mirroring.

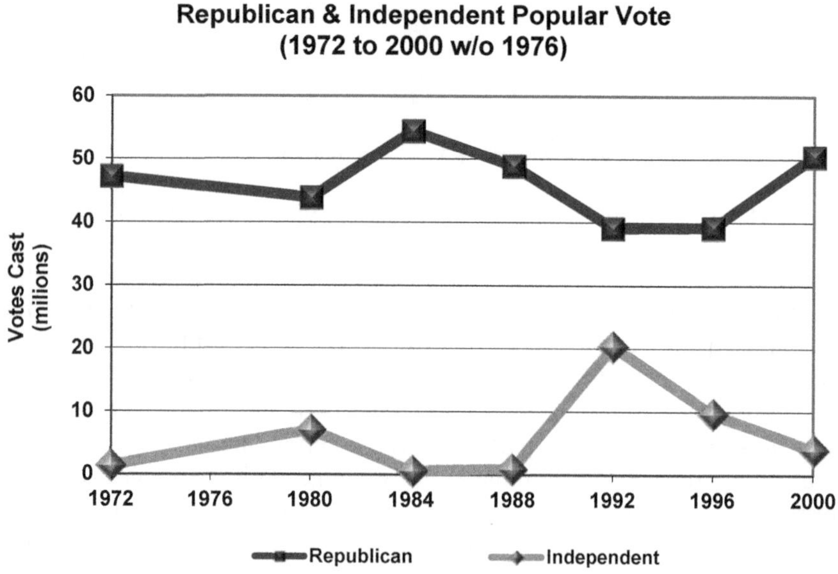

**Republican & Independent Popular Vote
(1972 to 2000 w/o 1976)**

Sources: US Census Bureau Statistical Abstracts 2004 and uselectionatlas.org

Figure 4-6 Republican & Independent Popular Vote
(1972 to 2000 w/o 1976)

However, since the Republican and Independent candidate voters were pulled from the same *pool* of voters, this unique circumstance should

---

[66] With the exception of a relatively small amount of voters.

have been visible when displayed on a graph. Thus, the first step in proving a relationship between the votes cast for the Republican and Independent candidates is to plot them on a line graph. Figure 4-6 displays these results. It depicts votes cast for the Republican and Independent candidates from 1972 to 2000. The emerging pattern is immediately apparent. The Republican popular vote is roughly a mirror image of the Independent candidates votes and vice versa.[67] Since the Republican or Independent candidates' voters may have chosen to not vote, the graph does not form an exact or ideal mirror image. Furthermore, the total votes cast fluctuate from election to election, which alters the mirroring of the two.

Furthermore, it is important to note that the mere existence of this mirror image brings additional validation to the trend theory. The mirroring could have only occurred if the Republican candidates and the Independent candidates were the only two jostling for the same pool of voters. If a third group, such as the Democratic candidates, were also fighting for the same pool of voters, the graph's image would have *not* been a mirror image.

Another method of viewing the relationship between the Republican and Independent voters is to view the corresponding increase or decrease from the previous election. As Table 4-3 demonstrates, a decrease in the Republican candidates votes from one year to another yield a corresponding increase for the Independent candidates votes.

Table 4-3 Increase or Decrease from Previous Election for Candidates in Presidential Elections, 1972 to 2000

	1972– 1980	1980– 1984	1984– 1988	1988– 1992	1992– 1996	1996– 2000
Republican	Decr	Incr	Decr	Decr	Incr	Incr
Independent	Incr	Decr	Incr	Incr	Decr	Decr
Democrat	Incr	Incr	Incr	Incr	Incr	Incr
Total Vote	Incr	Incr	Decr	Incr	Decr	Incr

Note: The election of 1976 is not included.

Source: US Census Bureau Statistical Abstracts 2004

---

[67] The deviating election of 1976 has been removed for clarity.

Alternatively, when the Republican votes cast increased, there is a corresponding decrease in the Independent candidates votes. Thus, Table 4-3 shows the inverse interconnectivity between the Republican and Independent candidates' votes cast. Also, the increase/decrease of the popular vote for Republican and Independent candidates, as well as the total popular vote, fluctuates from 1972 to 2000.

On the other hand, votes cast for the Democratic candidates only produce an increase from the previous election. As a matter of fact, the Democratic popular vote has increased not only every election from 1972 to 2000 (excluding 1976). The steady increase is the result of the linear trend of the Democratic candidate.

Furthermore, if we modify Fig. 4-6 by removing the 1992 election, where there was unusually high turnout activity of Independent voters, the graph images become remarkably mirrored (see Fig. 4-7).

Republican & Independent Popular Vote
(1972 to 2000 w/o 1976 & 1992)

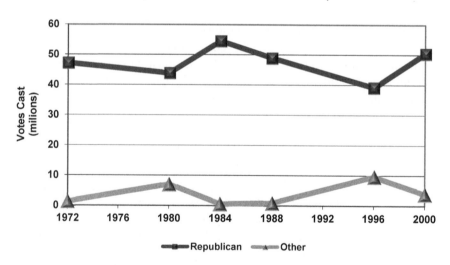

Sources: US Census Bureau Statistical Abstracts 2004 and uselectionatlas.org

Figure 4-7 Republican & Independent Popular Vote
(1972 to 2000, w/o 1976 & 1992)

The election in 1992, when Ross Perot performed so well as an Independent, brought in a substantial amount of new voters who did not vote in the previous election. This unusual voting activity of 1992[68] distorted the mirroring relationship.

Nonetheless, the graph in Fig. 4-7 exemplifies the relationship between the Republican and Independent candidates' popular vote. This is to say that when the Republican popular vote increased, the Independent candidates votes decreased a proportional amount. Likewise, when the Independent candidates votes increased the Republican votes decreased. When graphed, the two produce a unique mirror image of each other. The graph becomes even more mirrored when the 1984 election is removed as well.

A Graphical Representation of the Fractured Electorate

When all three types of voters are combined into one graph, the image provides a representation of the fractured electorate (see Fig. 4-8). That is to say that the Democratic candidate's votes increase in a linear manner while the Republican and Independent votes mirror each other. Also reflected with the graph is that the Democratic votes were not affected by either the Republican candidate's votes or the Independent candidate's votes.

The graph embodies the theory of the fractured electorate. The Democratic votes increase in a linear manner because it is theoretically isolated in a separate electorate (the Democratic electorate) with only or mostly Democratic voters. On the other hand, the Republican and Independent popular vote mirror each other because these two types of voters are the only voters contained in the non-Democratic electorate. Finally, the increase or decrease of Republican and Independent votes seems to not influence the Democratic candidate's votes due to the two existing in separate theoretical electorates. All in all, this graph proves to be an excellent single representation of what occurred to the voting electorate at the presidential level. It truly personifies the essence of the presidential trend.

---

[68] See Chapter 6.

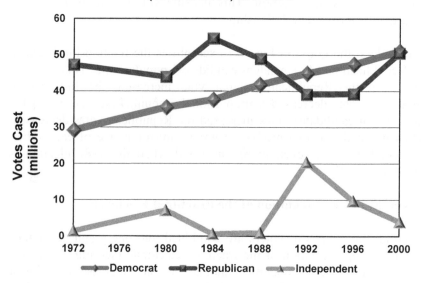

Figure 4-8 Democratic, Republican & Independent Popular Vote
(1972 to 2000, w/o 1976)

Chapter 5

The Reagan Non-Democrats

Introduction

Much has been said and written about the Reagan Democrats. Countless reports and analysis have been developed as well as debated. In most circumstances, the Reagan Democrats have been assumed to be actual Democratic voters. [69] However, did the theory of trend modify this common belief of Reagan Democrats?

The Reagan Non-Democrats

There is no question that Ronald Reagan garnered an exceptionally large amount of votes in 1984. In that year, Reagan obtained the third highest votes for president[70] in US history. However, did Reagan garner votes from Democratic voters in 1980 and in 1984?

If the trend theory is applied, the Democratic votes obtained by Reagan were not from the Democratic electorate[71]. In so far as the presidential level, they were from the non-Democratic electorate, and thus they were non-Democrats. The reason why many analysts classify those voters as Democrats is mostly due to the 1976 election. However, as discussed in Chap. 2, the 1976 election was a *deviating* election ... an anomaly. In

---

[69] The most important aspect to the Regan Democrats is that these voters included southern Democrats in addition to northern blue-collar workers and their children.

[70] In 2004, George W. Bush obtained the highest popular vote; John F. Kerry obtained the second highest.

[71] The Democratic Electorate includes those voters who vote for the Democratic candidate for president (see Chapter 4).

essence, these non-Democrats came back into the fold, if you will, for one election: 1976. The reality is that most had left the Democratic electorate back in 1968/1972. Thus, in fact, Reagan received votes from these new non-Democratic voters. It is important to note, once again, that this referred to Democratic voters related to presidential elections not elections for other offices.

Democratic, Republican & Independet Popular Vote (1972 to 2000)

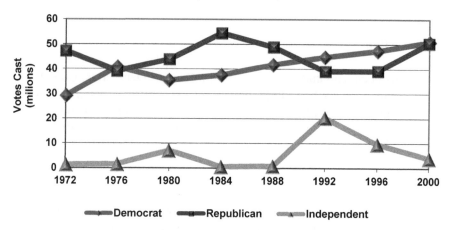

Sources: US Census Bureau Statistical Abstracts 2004 and uselectionatlas.org

Figure 5-1 Democratic, Republican & Independent Popular Vote (1972 to 2000)

Proof of Reagan not acquiring Democratic voters from the Democratic electorate lies with the trend itself. If Reagan obtained Democratic votes, there would have been an appreciable decrease in the presidential trend line. As Fig. 5-1 shows, there is no appreciable decrease in the presidential trend in 1980 or 1984.

Again, the standard assumption is that since Jimmy Carter, in 1980, received less votes than he did in 1976, Reagan pulled Democratic voters away from Carter. This seemed reasonable unless you consider the presidential trend theory. It is true that Reagan pulled votes away from Carter; however, the election of 1976 is an anomaly. The additional voters who Jimmy Carter received in 1976 were only there for a single election and did not return to vote for a Democratic candidate for president for at least the next three decades. Thus, it is true that Reagan received the Jimmy Carter Democrats.

For quantifiable evidence, Chap. 7 will provide analysis that compared a trend line of the Democratic candidate's votes cast to the actual votes obtained. Although exit polls show that a certain amount of Democratic voters swung back and forth between the Democratic candidates and the Republican candidates (see Table 13-2), the true test is whether the trend is altered from its normal trajectory. The trend is not modified substantially from its normal trend line.

Hence, in 1984, the Democratic candidate received less than 800,000 votes than the trend line predicted (see Chap. 7).[72] If all of these voters came from the Democratic electorate, Reagan received less than 800,000 more votes from the Democratic side (out of his total of 54 million votes). Thus, less than 1.5 percent of Reagan's popular vote came from the new Reagan Democrats that added to the normal trend line.

Consequently, considering the trend, the vast majority of perceived Democratic voters who voted for Ronald Reagan were not true Democratic voters (at the presidential level). They were mostly non-Democrats who had left the Democratic electorate in 1968 or at least in 1972. Hence Reagan received votes from those who voted for Carter in 1976, but those voters were most likely non-Democrats.

---

[72] In 1980, the Democratic candidate received 200,000 more than the Democratic trend line estimated. In this scenario, conceptually, Reagan did not obtain any Reagan Democrats.

The Reagan Non-Democrats

Chapter 6

The Baseline Trends

Introduction

Many original theories spawn additional supplemental ones. The presidential trend is no different. By observing that the trend centers on voters repeatedly voting for the Democratic candidate, these voters, in essence, constitute the *core* or *base* voters. Tracking these core or base voters from election to election form what could be called a "baseline trend," which outlines the growth of the core voters from election to election. After 1972, the popular voter for the Democratic candidate consisted mostly of its core voters. Hence, it was principally the Democratic baseline trend. [73] But what about the Republican or Independent candidate's baseline?

Although the baseline trend theory focuses on core or base voters, it was determined by exit poll analysis that it also included a consistent group of *swing voters* (see Chap. 13 "Analysis of the Trend Using Exit Polls"). Nonetheless, the baseline trend appears to be an offshoot or even a precursor to the presidential trend and remains such an oddity that it needed to be covered and explored this book.

A Baseline Trend?

The previous graph presented in Chap. 4, which depicts the Republican and Independent candidates, reveals another peculiarity besides the

---

[73] The linear baseline trend for the Democratic candidates could also be perceived as an upper limit trend. This is due to the probable existence of a maximum amount of voters that crossover from the non-Democratic electorate to vote for the Democratic candidate.

mirror effect (see Fig. 6-1). The mirror effect in Chap. 4 shows that the graphs of Republican and Independent votes were close to mirror images of each other. The election on the graph that did *not* follow the mirror pattern was in 1992. When considering the additional voters that *turned out* to vote for Ross Perot in 1992, there should have been a greater decrease for the votes for George H. W. Bush (see Fig. 6-1). It was as if the popular vote for Bush collided with some type of *floor* that did not allow his popular vote to go any lower. Was there something that prevented the Republican vote from dipping lower? The answer is similar to the Democratic candidate's trend after 1972. There was another group of voters that only voted for the Republican Party's candidate, the *Republican* core or base voters.

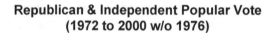

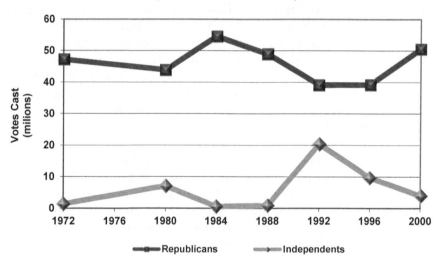

Sources: US Census Bureau Statistical Abstracts 2004 and uselectionatlas.org

Figure 6-1 Republican & Independent's Popular Vote
(1972 to 2000 w/o 1976)

Intuitively, it makes sense that if there were voters that only or mostly voted for the Democratic candidate, there should be voters who only or mostly vote for the Republican candidates. Consequently, just as the presidential trend consists of these core Democratic voters, there exists a Republican trend made up of Republican voters as well. However, according to the trend theory, the Republican voters are part of the non-Democratic electorate that only contains Republican and Independent voters (see Chap. 4). Hence, most of the time the Republican popular vote had additional non-majority party voters added to the popular vote that masked the Republican baseline trend. However, in 1992 the number of core Republican voters revealed themselves by showing that the votes for Bush did not dip lower as expected (according to the mirror effect). However, how could the remaining core Republican baseline trend be revealed given that the Republican popular vote included non-majority party voters? As with the 1992 election, there should be a way to strip away the non-majority party voters to reveal the Republican base voters.

First, an explanation for the 1992 anomaly is developed. It is first determined that since the 1992 election included a non-majority party candidate, Ross Perot, that garnered an extraordinary amount of votes, the remaining voters in the non-Democratic electorate were Republican core voters. These core Republican voters essentially always voted for the Republican candidate. Thus, the non-majority party candidates could have only taken away a maximum amount of voters from the Republican candidate before reaching the core voters. This is the reason why the votes for George H. W. Bush in 1992 were not lower than expected given the mirror effect. In subsequent exit poll analysis, it is determined that the core or base voters were not the only voters preventing the mirror effect of 1992 (see below, "Defining the Baseline").

Second, if at least two other elections had a sizeable amount of votes cast for the non-majority party candidates, it may duplicate what occurred in 1992. These two additional elections, along with the 1992 election, could be graphed to determine if a Republican's baseline trend can be revealed. The central assumption is that if the popular votes cast for the Democratic core aligned itself along a straight line, because of linear population growth, so should the Republican core voters. Three elections were needed to reveal the Republican core baseline vote trend. Two elections would produce a line, but three are required to display the minimum for a trend. Since the 1992 election had already been discovered, there is a need to find only two others.

The second election was quickly determined. It was the year that the electorate was fractured, 1968. Remember, the criteria is to find an election whereby the Independent candidate obtained a substantial amount of votes. In 1968, George Wallace received a substantial amount of votes as an Independent Party candidate. Wallace received over 9.9 million votes and over 13.5 percent of the popular vote. Consequently, Wallace obtained the largest popular vote, at that time, for a third party candidate since 1924.

The third election meets the criteria as well. Reviewing the non-majority party votes cast for the election of 1948 made it stand out. In 1948, Governor James "Strom" Thurman ran for president under a new third party called the States' Rights or Dixiecrat Party. Yes, this was the same Strom Thurman who ended up being the long serving senator from South Carolina. In addition, the Dixiecrats consisted mostly of individuals who splintered off from the Democratic Party because of the support that the party had for several controversial civil rights planks. If this sounds familiar to you, it should be. It seems similar to the 1968 election. However, it was prior to 1968, so it was not a repeat, it was actually foreshadowing.

Thus, three elections existed that met the criteria to prove the baseline trend hypothesis. The best way to view the results is to plot these elections on a graph. Therefore, the popular vote for the Republican candidates for the elections years of 1948, 1968, and 1992 are plotted. The results are shown in Fig. 6-2.

Once again, votes cast remarkably seem to align themselves in a near straight line (see Chap. 9 to review measures of *linearity* for the Republican baseline trend). After it is determined that all of these elections were aligned, the question arises: What about the Democratic and Independent Party candidates and what would those same three elections show if they were plotted on the same graph? Thus, the votes cast for the Democratic and Independent Party candidates are added to the graph. Again, the graph reveals a remarkably linear trend (see Fig. 6-3). However, not just for the Republican votes cast, but for the Democratic and Independent candidate's votes as well.

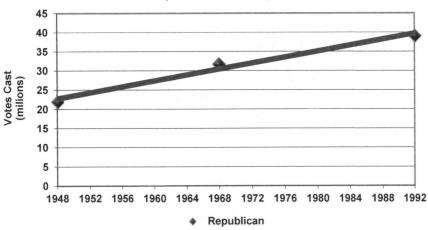

Sources: US Census Bureau Statistical Abstracts 1942 to 2001 and uselectionatlas.org

Figure 6-2 Republican Popular Vote
(1948, 1968, 1992)

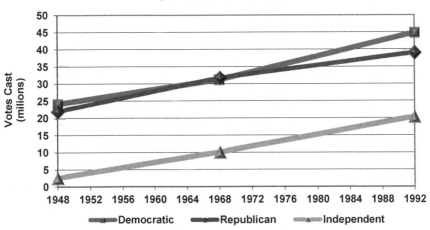

Sources: US Census Bureau Statistical Abstracts 1942 to 2001 and uselectionatlas.org

Figure 6-3 Democratic/Republican/Independent Popular Vote
(1948, 1968, 1992)

It is noticed that the Democratic and Republican baseline trends are not as linear as the Independent candidates are.[74] The Democratic baseline seems to bend upward while the Republican baseline tilts downward from 1968 to 1992. Discussion of this shifting is covered later in this chapter (see below, "The New Democratic Baseline").

However, regardless of the tilting, the fact that each of the political groups aligns themselves using the same three elections is more than a mere coincidence. Something had to have occurred at those three elections. Given these results, an explanation for this unique anomaly needed to be developed.

The Root Cause of the Baseline Trend

One of the starting points to begin defining the root cause of this voting peculiarity is the criteria that is used in selecting the elections. The central criterion is a substantial amount of votes *for* the Independent candidate. The other criterion is an angered portion of the electorate that backed the Independent Party candidate.

Hence, in each of these elections, there was a substantial Independent candidate. The second criterion is that Independent candidate garnered votes from a disgruntled population for some particular volatile issue or issues. The issues were polarizing enough that, for the most part, only the core voters diverged to their respective major party affiliation. The essential ingredient that left the core voters for the two major parties to reveal themselves was a significant Independent candidate. The Independent candidate in each of the three elections attracted the remaining voters, who were not core or base voters, away from the other major parties. However, in order for the Independent candidates to draw a substantial amount of voters, there needed to be some major issue or issues that were unsettling enough for the noncore voters to shift over. To illustrate this scenario, consider the three elections.

First, reviewing the election in 1948, the Democratic President Harry S. Truman issued two executive orders that were controversial for their time: banning segregation in the armed forces and guaranteeing fair

---

[74] The r^2 values of the Democratic, Republican, and Independent baselines are .9837, .9817, and .9987, respectively.

employment practices in civil service. The initiatives may not be so controversial in more modern times but were extremely controversial in the 1940s. These initiatives made President Truman the first president to address civil rights issues for African Americans since Abraham Lincoln.[75] Although the military took two years to implement the law, his initiatives did not sit well with some individuals, including some Democrats. Specifically, the Democrats in the South were especially angered by these initiatives.

Some southern Democrats were so outraged by Truman's executive orders that it became one of the central impetuses for a group of delegates during the 1948 Democratic National Convention to splinter off and form the States' Rights or Dixiecrat Party.[76] The new Dixiecrat Party nominated a young governor named James "Strom" Thurman. That year in 1948, Governor Thurman received over 1.1 million votes or 2.4 percent of the popular vote.[77] Although Thurman received what was perceived as a relatively small amount, it caused the first fissure in the electorate that was to completely fracture in 1968 to 1972 (see Chap. 2).

Next, in 1968, the election that began the fracturing of the electorate, the Democratic President was Lyndon Johnson and the disgruntled Democratic governor from Alabama was George Wallace. Like Strom Thurman, George Wallace ran for president under a new third party. The new third party, called the American Independent Party, was adamantly opposed to the series of civil rights laws that had previously passed. Touting "states' rights"[78] and select "working-class or blue collar" issues George Wallace received over 9.9 million votes or 13.5 percent of the popular vote.[79]

The third and final baseline point, 1992, featured a different incumbent party, a significant Independent, and different issues. Yet the theme was

---

[75] Michael R. Gardner, *Harry Truman and Civil Rights: Moral Courage and Political Risks*, Southern Illinois University Press, 2002

[76] Kari Frederickson, *The Dixiecrat Revolt and the End of the Solid South, 1932-1968*, University of North Carolina Press, 2001

[77] US Census Bureau, Statistical Abstract of the US, 1951

[78] Yanek Mieczkowski, *The Routledge Historical Atlas of Presidential Elections*, Routledge, 2001

[79] US Census Bureau, Statistical Abstract of the US, 1970

essentially the same. This election included a Republican president, George Herbert Walker Bush. The Independent candidate running was billionaire Henry "Ross" Perot. The election this time did not include a disgruntled Democrat opposed to civil rights. It included a disgruntle billionaire, Ross Perot[80], and associated voters who were opposed to the soaring national debt and annual deficit.[81] They were also displeased with President Bush's reversal on "no new taxes." Perot performed exceptionally well and received 19.7 million votes or 18.9 percent of the popular vote.[82]

Thus, each three elections (1948, 1968, and 1992) consisted of a substantial Independent candidate and one or more volatile issues. The volatile issues enabled the Independent candidates to obtain a substantial amount of votes. These elections reflected an alignment of voters to their respective political party and produced the anomaly, the baseline trend.

The Republican Baseline Evidence

As covered in Chap. 4, the existence of the Republican baseline was *detectable* by the *non-mirror* image of the 1992 election. For the most part, the Republican and Independent candidates' popular vote displayed a pattern of mirroring each other. The increase in the Independent candidates vote produced a relatively similar decrease in the Republican vote in all elections from 1972 to 2000, except for 1992 (excluding 1976)

Figure 6-4 reveals that the 1992 election with Ross Perot's exceptional popular vote (included in the Independent candidate's vote) did not yield a similar magnitude of decline in the Republican's votes. The potential reason for the disproportionate decline mostly lies with the Republican baseline. If the baseline trend truly existed, the total votes for the Republican candidate should never decrease appreciably lower than the baseline amount. As Fig. 6-6 shows, evidence for the Democratic candidates, Fig. 6-5 indicates this was also true for the Republican candidates.

---

[80] Yanek Mieczkowski, *The Routledge Historical Atlas of Presidential Elections*, Routledge, 2001

[81] At one point, Ross Perot purchased television airtime to discuss the national debt and deficit in the form of an infomercial.

[82] US Census Bureau, *Statistical Abstract of the US*, 1994

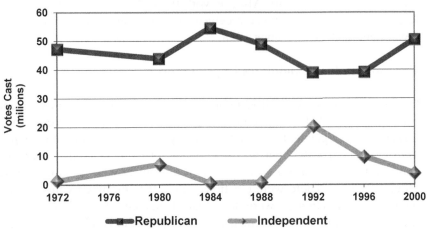

Sources: US Census Bureau Statistical Abstracts 2004 and uselectionatlas.org

Figure 6-4 Republican & Independent Popular Vote
(1972 to 2000, w/o 1976)

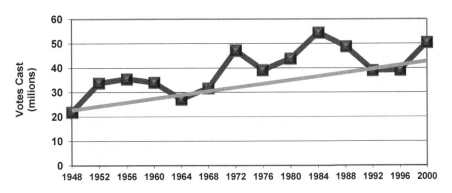

Sources: US Census Bureau Statistical Abstracts 1951 to 2006 and uselectionatlas.org

Figure 6-5 Republican Baseline Trend/Popular Vote
(1948 to 2000)

Therefore, in 1992, Ross Perot had reached the maximum limit of Republican voters (that usually turnout) that could be pulled away from the Republican candidate. Also, as with the Democratic candidates, the Republican candidates never received an appreciable amount of votes fewer than the baseline since 1948.

The Independent Candidates Upper Limit

Unlike the Democratic and Republican baseline trends, the Independent candidates' trend did not represent a minimum amount of votes cast. Instead the Independent candidates' trend provided a maximum or *upper limit* number of votes that was obtainable. The Independent candidates could not have a baseline because they did not possess a core or base group of voters. There were elections where the combined votes for the independent candidates were less than 1 percent. In addition, many Independent voters mostly voted for the Republican candidates. Finally, if a core or base did exist, it was so small that it remained insignificant for the purpose of this book.

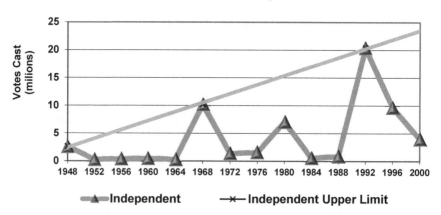

Figure 6-6 Independent Upper Limit/Popular Vote
(1948 to 2000)

As Fig. 6-6 displays, the Independent candidates had not received total votes greater than the upper limit trend. As a consequence, the Independent candidates had the reverse effect of the major party candidates. This is to say that the Independent votes never received more votes than the upper limit.

The New Democratic Baseline: A Shift in 1972

Although the Democratic and Republican baseline trend closely aligned itself with the 1948, 1968, and 1992 elections, there seems to have been a minor shift from 1968 to 1992 (see Fig. 6-7). At the same time, the Independent baseline does not appear to upward as with the Democratic or even Republican baseline.

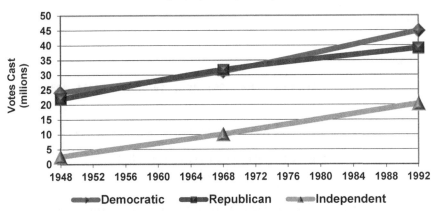

Democratic, Republican & Independent Baseline (1948, 1968, 1992)

Sources: US Census Bureau Statistical Abstracts 1942 to 2001 and uselectionatlas.org

Figure 6-7 Democratic, Republican, Independent Baseline (1948, 1968, 1992)

The key to solving why the Democratic and Republican baseline does not align perfectly resides in the 1972 election. The Democratic candidate's vote in the 1972 election dips lower than that of the 1968 election. If the Democratic baseline truly existed, votes cast in 1972 should not have been lower than the 1968 election. That is true unless the fracturing of the electorate was not complete until 1972. This seems to be the case.

In 1968, there remained some Democratic voters who apparently voted for Hubert Humphrey; however, in 1972, they *broke-off*. For more detailed data on the shift, review Chap. 9.

Apparently, the fracturing began in 1968 and was completed in 1972 when the Democratic Electorate essentially became the core or base voters (Fig. 6-8). The breach of the Democratic baseline created a new Democratic baseline. After 1972, these core voters produced the linear presidential trend.

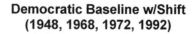

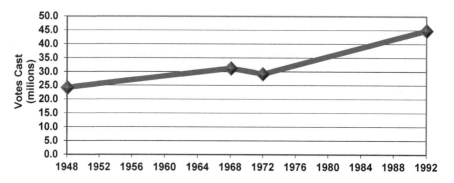

Sources: US Census Bureau Statistical Abstracts 1942 to 2001 and uselectionatlas.org

Figure 6-8 Democratic Baseline w/Shift
(1948, 1968, 1972, 1992)

Evidence of the new baseline can be seen in the graph shown in Fig. 6-9. Votes cast for the Democratic candidates did not dip appreciably below the old and new baselines from 1948 to 2000. The fact that the Democratic votes do not dip below the baseline corroborates the theory that the baseline consisted mostly of core voters.

As displayed on the graph, the actual baseline trend of the Democratic candidates' dips from 1968 to 1972, but then continues to rise in a linear manner to 2000.

Essentially, a new baseline is created for 1972 that drops lower than the baseline from 1948 to 1968. Hence, the reason why the Democratic baseline of 1948, 1968, and 1992 is not as linear as the Independent baselines is due to this dip in the base voters. This crack creates a shift upward in the Democratic baseline and the presidential trend.

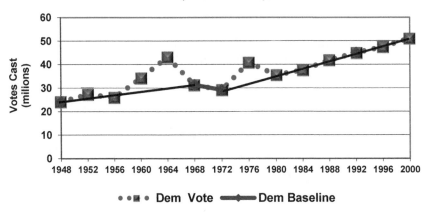

**Democratic Popular Vote/Baseline w/Shift
(1948 to 2000)**

● ●■ ● **Dem Vote** ━━◆━━**Dem Baseline**

Sources: US Census Bureau Statistical Abstracts 1951 to 2004 and uselectionatlas.org

Figure 6-6 Democratic Popular Vote/Baseline w/Shift
(1948 to 2000)

A Non-Democratic Shift in 1972

It stands to reason that a shift in the Democratic baseline from 1968 to 1972 would result in an increase in the Republican or non-Democratic voting electorate. If additional voters broke off from the Democratic electorate from 1968 to 1972, they must have gone somewhere. Either they became part of those who never vote or they became part of the Republican or non-Democratic electorate.

However, the shift in the Republican baseline would not be visible. The reason lies with the Republican vote partially consisting of Independent voters, specifically in 1972. The voters who voted for the Independent candidate shifted to the Republican candidate in 1972. Therefore, if there were a Republican baseline shift, it would be masked by additional Independent voters.

Nonetheless, the non-Democratic baseline may show a shift. Thus, if a graph is produced of the Democratic and non-Democratic (Republican plus Independent) baselines with 1972 added, the results may show a shift (see Fig. 6-10). As Fig. 6-10 displays, from 1968 to 1972 the presidential trend *tilts* downward and a corresponding non-Democrat trend bends upward. See Chap. 9 for statistical analysis of the shift in the baseline trends.

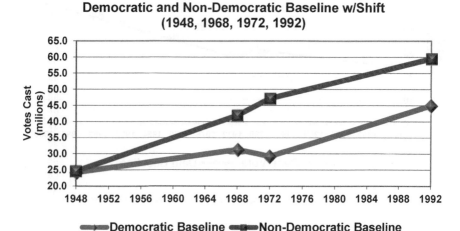

Sources: US Census Bureau Statistical Abstracts 1951 to 2004 and uselectionatlas.org

Figure 6-10 Democratic/Non-Dem Baseline w/Shift
(1948, 1968, 1972, 1992)

Since the non-Democratic baseline consisted of summing the Republican baseline and the Independent upper limit, the combination is actually a hybrid. The Republican baseline that provided the *floor* or minimum amount of votes that a Republican candidate should make. While the Independent upper limit trend provided the maximum amount of votes that an Independent candidate could pull from the major party candidates.

However, when the non-Democratic votes are graphed, they appear to show a near upper limit of votes cast (see Fig. 6-11). Every election from 1948 to 2000, except for 1952 and 1956, resides below the non-presidential trend line. Hence, the elections of 1948, 1968, 1972, and 1992 form, for the most part, the non-Democratic upper-limit trend line.

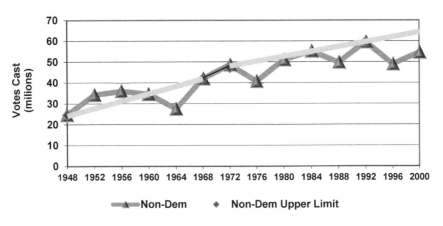

Sources: US Census Bureau Statistical Abstracts 1951 to 2006 and uselectionatlas.org

Figure 6-11 Non-Democratic Popular Vote/Upper Limit w/Shift
(1948 to 2000)

The Baseline Trends

PART 2

Trend Analysis

Chapter 7

Proving the Phenomenon

Introduction

In order to completely prove that the linear presidential trend existed, it should be quantified in some manner. Therefore, in this chapter numerical values are calculated and analyzed to validate the linearity and thus the predictability of the popular vote for the Democratic candidates. It is important to note that some table decimal values have been rounded and may differ slightly from the readers final calculated values.

Predictable Trend Since 1980

Since the predictable trend, from 1972 to 2000, included a *deviating* election in 1976, we will first analyze the segment of the presidential trend that did not include that particular election. Therefore, the votes cast in each of the presidential elections since 1980 are analyzed. Table 7-1 contains the votes cast for the Democrat, Republican, and Independent candidates since 1980. Figure 7-1 presents the same data in a bar chart graphical format.

Table 7-1 Popular Vote in Presidential Elections,
1980 to 2000
(millions)

	1980	1984	1988	1992	1996	2000
Democrat	35.5	37.6	41.8	44.9	47.4	51.0
Republican	43.9	54.5	48.9	39.1	39.2	50.5
Non-Major	7.1	0.6	0.9	20.4	9.7	4.0

Sources: US Census Bureau Statistical Abstracts 1951 to 2006 and uselectionatlas.org

Note: The values have been rounded to the nearest single decimal point.

93

Figure 7-1 indicates that the popular vote for the Republican and Independent candidates has fluctuated up and down since 1980 while the votes for the Democratic candidate have steadily increased. Not only has the popular vote for the Democratic candidate increased in every election since 1980, after a close inspection, it appears to have increased in a linear fashion.

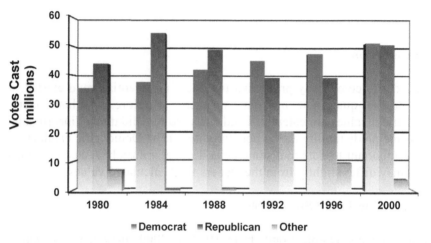

Sources: US Census Bureau Statistical Abstracts 1951 to 2006 and uselectionatlas.org

Figure 7-1 Democratic, Republican & Independent Popular Vote
(1980 to 2000)

Thus, the popular vote for the Democratic candidate follows along a straight line from the 1980 election to the 2000 election. The linear aspect of the popular vote may not have been apparent until displayed in a scatter graph format. For clarity, Fig. 7-2 displays a scatter graph of only the votes cast for the Democratic candidate from 1980 to 2000.

By simply glancing at Fig. 7-2, votes cast appear to have increased in a linear fashion. However, in order to truly determine if the votes cast were linear, the correlation value between the increase in votes cast and the increase in election years should be measured (since each year should provide an equal increase in votes cast). In essence, measure how close votes cast follow a straight line.

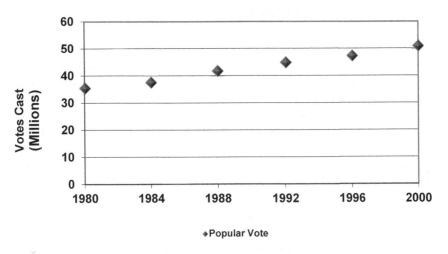

Democratic Popular Vote
(1980 to 2000)

Sources: US Census Bureau Statistical Abstracts 1951 to 2006 and uselectionatlas.org

Figure 7-2 Democratic Popular Vote
(1980 to 2000)

The most common measurement for correlations is called the "correlation coefficient." The correlation coefficient measures the degree and direction of linear relationship between two variables.[83] The most common correlation coefficient is referred to by r. It is important to note that the use of correlation is simply used as a value to determine linearity, not to determine whether or not there is a correlation.

Another, and sometimes more useful indicator, is calculated by squaring r. This is called the "coefficient of determination," "R-squared" or r^2. The r^2 presents a measurement of the proportion of the variation that one variable can be accounted for by the other. In other words, r^2 measures how well a linear regression line represents the data or, in this case, how well it follows the perfect presidential trend line. In this instance, using the votes cast for the Democratic candidate in relationship to the presidential election years from 1980 to 2000, the r^2 squared is calculated to be .994. An r^2 value of 1.00 has a perfect positive correlation and

---

[83] A perfect correlation is has an r of 1.00 and an r^2 of 1.00.

follows along a straight line. Since an r^2 value greater than .8 usually indicates a strong or high correlation, votes cast for the Democratic candidate reflect high correlation.

Because the election year is used in the correlation, the popular vote actually correlated with *a perfectly linear increase* from election year to election year (since the presidency is selected every four years). Once again, in this instance, it is important to note that this is simply a measurement of the linearity or straightness of the line. It is not, necessarily, a correlation between two variables. When the r^2 of the Democratic popular vote and the voting age population from 1972 to 2000 are compared, it calculates to a value of .976. When correlated with the number of registered voters, it yields an impressive .974.

Voting age population and registered voters are useful for determining a correlation between the Democratic popular vote and those two attributes. However, when determining how linear or straight the presidential trend was, using the election years is the best comparison. This particular instance it is not significant that the values be tremendously accurate (ex. .997 versus .974). The most important aspect of this theory is not the specific values of the trend lines, but that the popular vote for Democratic candidate for president trends in an extremely predictable pattern for almost 30 years.

To illustrate how impressively strong this correlation is, compare the same correlation for the popular vote for the Republican and Independent candidates. The r^2 value for votes cast for the Republican candidate from 1980 to 2000 is calculated to be an unimpressive .037. The r^2 value for the votes cast for the Independent candidates is almost as bad at .049.

A second method of proving the linearity of the election points is to compare the actual data with the estimated results of a linear *regression line*. [84] The regression line is the closest line that best fits all data points. Since the regression line is a straight line, it appears in the form of a standard line equation:

$$PV = bx + a$$

---

[84] The least-squares method of calculating the regression equation is used.

The variable *PV* represents the popular vote for the Democratic candidate while *x* is the presidential election year. The constant *a* is the value of *y* if *x* is zero.[85] The constant *b* represents the slope of the line.

Using votes cast along with the election years from 1980 to 2000, the equation[86] that depicts the regression line is determined to be:

$$PV = .78706x - 1523.21$$

where *PV* is the popular vote and *x* is the election year.

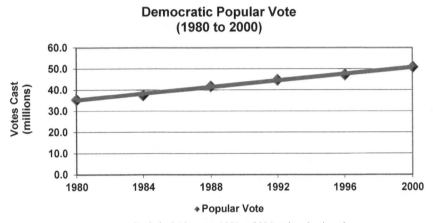

Sources: US Census Bureau Statistical Abstracts 1951 to 2006 and uselectionatlas.org

Figure 7-3 Democratic Popular Vote
(1980 to 2000)

Using the above equation and substituting the appropriate year, estimates of the actual votes cast are calculated. Table 7-2 displays the results of actual votes cast along with the values calculated using the regression equation. In addition, accuracy of estimated votes cast is calculated to determine the how close the regression line matches the actual election points (100% – absolute value [actual – estimated]/divided by the actual

---

[85] Since *x* does not begin with 0 election year, the *Y* intercept assumes an election year of 1980 instead of the typical 0.

[86] The derived equation depends upon the specific popular vote used to calculate the regression line.

value). The level of accuracy of the estimated value ranges from a maximum of 99.6 percent to a minimum of 96.6 percent. It is clear that votes cast for the Democratic candidate had progressed in a consistent linear trend from 1980 to 2000.

Table 7-2 Popular Vote for the Democratic Candidate and Estimated Amount, 1980 to 2000
(millions)

	1980	1984	1988	1992	1996	2000
Democrat	35.5	37.6	41.8	44.9	47.4	51.0
Trend Line Estimate (1980 to 2004)	35.2	38.3	41.5	44.6	47.8	50.9
Accuracy, %	96.6	99.0	99.6	99.1	96.7	96.8

Sources: US Census Bureau Statistical Abstracts 1951 to 2006 and uselectionatlas.org

Note: Values are rounded to the nearest single decimal point. See Appendix B for actual values used in the calculations.

Predictable Trend Since 1972

The next step is to statistically prove whether the predictable trend extended to the election of 1972. However, the 1976 election will be removed from the calculations because it has been designated a deviating election and will be treated as an outlier.[87]

Table 7-3 Popular Vote in Presidential Elections, 1972 to 2000
(millions)

	1972	1980	1984	1988	1992	1996	2000
Democrat	29.2	35.5	37.6	41.8	44.9	47.4	51.0
Republican	47.2	43.9	54.5	48.9	39.1	39.2	50.5
Non-Major	1.4	7.1	0.6	0.9	20.4	9.7	4.0

Sources: US Census Bureau Statistical Abstracts 1951 to 2006 and uselectionatlas.org

As before, the popular vote, this time since 1972, is reviewed and presented in tabular and graphical forms (see Table 7-3 and Fig. 7-4).

---

[87] Outliers are individual points that are substantially greater or smaller than the other values in a data set. In many instances, outliers are eliminated from the data set in order to not skew the analysis.

The graph in Fig. 7-4 clearly shows that votes cast for Republican and Independent candidates show no obvious consistent trend throughout the elections of 1972 to 2000. However, votes cast in 1972 for the Democratic candidate appear to be aligned with the elections of 1980 through 2000.

Democratic, Republican & Independent Popular Vote (1972 to 2000 w/o 1976)

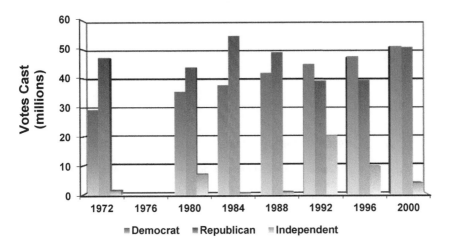

Sources: US Census Bureau Statistical Abstracts 1951 to 2006 and uselectionatlas.org

Figure 7-4 Democratic, Republican, Independent Popular Vote (1972 to 2000, w/o 1976)

In fact, when the regression equation for the election years of 1972 to 2000 is recalculated, it yields similar results as the 1980 trend. The new regression equation for 1972 through 2000 becomes:

$$PV = 77848x - 1506.12$$

where *PV* is the popular vote and *x* is the election year.

Nonetheless, the consistent trend of votes cast can be easily identified in Fig. 7-5 when the data is viewed as a line graph compared with the regression line. Table 7-4 includes the results of actual votes cast along with the values calculated using the new regression formula. As before, the deviation between the actual votes cast and the estimated votes cast can be calculated to determine the accuracy of the formula.

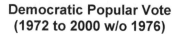

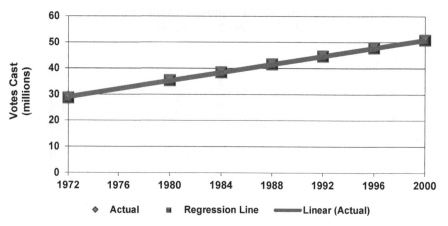

Sources: US Census Bureau Statistical Abstracts 1951 to 2006 and uselectionatlas.org

Figure 7-5 Democratic Popular Vote
(1972 to 2000, w/o 1976)

The highest accuracy between the actual and the regression line, ranges from a maximum of 99.6 percent to a low of 95.2 percent. When the r^2 value is calculated, from 1972 to 2000, it is determined to be .997. Again, a value of 1 is considered a perfectly straight line. Additional proof of how linear the popular vote for the Democratic candidate was resides with comparing votes cast with two additional voting related data.

Table 7-4 Popular Vote for Democratic Candidate in Presidential Elections and Predicted Amount, 1972 to 2000
(millions)

	1972	1980	1984	1988	1992	1996	2000
Democrat	29.2	35.5	37.6	41.8	44.9	47.4	51.0
Estimate (1972 to 2000)	29.0	35.3	38.4	41.5	44.6	47.7	50.8
Accuracy, %	95.2	99.4	97.9	99.2	99.3	99.3	99.7

Sources: US Census Bureau Statistical Abstracts 1951 to 2006 and uselectionatlas.org

There is one additional example of the linearity of the trend. When the presidential trend is compared with the trend of the voting age population as well as the number of registered voters, the presidential trend is *more* linear. Visually, the presidential trend appears to be a much straighter trend line than the other two (see Fig. 7-6). Indeed, when the r^2 value is calculated, the presidential trend amount is .997 while the registered voter is .971 and the voting age population is .969.

Dem. Popular Vote, VAP and Reg. Voters Trend Lines (1972 to 2000 w/o 1976)

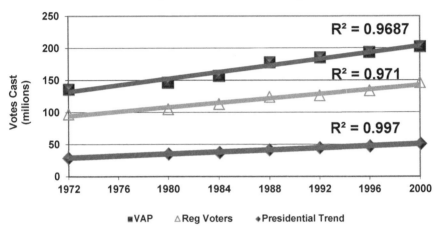

Source: US Census Bureau Statistical Abstracts 1951 to 2006 and uselectionatlas.org

Figure 7-6 Democratic Popular Vote/VAP/Registered Voter Trend Lines (1972 to 2000)

The fact that the presidential trend is more linear than the trend of voting age population or registered voters was amazing. With all of the different variables involved, how could the vote for the Democratic candidates be more stable than the increase in voting age population and registered voters? The answer of course is the fracturing of our electorate.

Proving the Phenomenon

Chapter 8

Projecting the Popular Vote

Introduction

Now that the popular vote for the Democratic candidate has been proven to be linear from 1972 to 2000,[88] the essential question still remains: could a projection or prediction of future votes cast could have been derived? In other words, if the trend line for previous popular vote results is extended, could it accurately predict future election amounts? This chapter investigates whether the presidential trend could have been used to project the popular vote of the next election four years earlier or even more.[89] Thus we put the presidential trend to test or, as William Whewell stated, "It is a test of true theories not only to account for but to predict phenomena."

Projecting the 1988 Election

In order to make a valid prediction, we need at least three elections to define the trend line. Consequently, the first projection would have been made for the 1988 election. As a result, the regression equation must be derived from the popular vote in the elections of 1972, 1980, and 1984. When calculated, the regression equation would be:

$$PV = 0.7129x - 1377$$

where PV is the popular vote and x is the election year.

---

[88] Excluding the 1976 election.
[89] The number of decimal places used for the slope (x) may change the popular vote estimate.

The results obtained by calculating the popular vote for the 1988 election using the above regression equation is presented in Table 8-1. The estimated votes cast are found to be 97.4 percent accurate.

Table 8-1 Democratic Popular Vote
and the Predicted Amount, 1988
(millions)

	1988
Democratic Popular Vote	41.8
Projection (1972 to 1984)	40.7
Accuracy, %	97.4

By determining the r^2 for votes cast from 1972, 1980, and 1984, an alternative measurement of the linearity is made. The r^2 for the votes cast is calculated to be .9906 (with the value of "1" being a perfectly straight line). Using the same regression equation, the 1992, 1996, and 2000 elections could have been predicted with 97.0, 98.0, and 96.5 percent accuracy, respectively.

Projecting the 1992 Election

The next election results that could have been predicted would have been for 1992. The regression equation derived from using the votes cast in the prior elections of 1972, 1980, 1984, and 1988 would have been:

$$PV = 0.767x - 1483$$

where PV is the popular vote and x is the election year.

The results obtained by calculating votes cast for the 1992 election using the above regression equation are presented in Table 8-2. The estimated votes cast are found to be 99.0 percent accurate.

The r^2 for votes cast from 1972 to 1992 is calculated to be .9940. Using the same regression equation, 1996 and 2000 elections could have been predicted with 99.7 and 99.1 percent accuracy, respectively. **In effect, the popular vote for the Democratic candidate could have been predicted in 1988 with an accuracy of 99% or better.**

	1992
Table 8-2 Democratic Popular Vote and the Predicted Amount, 1992 (millions)	
Democratic Popular Vote	44.9
Projection (1972 to 1988)	44.4
Accuracy, %	99.0

Projecting the 1996 Election

The regression equation derived using the popular vote for the elections of 1972, 1980, 1984, 1988, and 1992 would be:

$$PV = 0.7841x - 1517$$

where PV is the popular vote and x is the election year.

The result obtained by calculating votes cast for the 1996 election using the above regression equation is presented in Table 8-3. The estimated votes cast are found to be 99.1 percent accurate.

	1996
Table 8-3 Democratic Popular Vote and the Predicted Amount, 1996 (millions)	
Democratic Popular Vote	47.4
Projection (1972 to 1992)	47.8
Accuracy, %	99.1

The r^2 for votes cast from 1972 to 1996 is calculated to be .9956. Using the same regression equation, the 2000 election could have been predicted with 99.9 percent accuracy.

Projecting the 2000 Election

Furthermore, the regression equation derived from using the popular vote for the elections of 1972, 1980, 1984, 1988, 1992, and 1996 would be:

$$PV = 0.7719x - 1493$$

where PV is the popular vote and x is the election year.

The results obtained by calculating votes cast for the 2000 election using the above regression equation are presented in Table 8-4. The estimated votes cast are found to be 99.43 percent accurate.

Table 8-4 Democratic Popular Vote and the Predicted Amount, 2000 (millions)	2000
Democratic Popular Vote	51.0
Projection (1972 to 1996)	50.7
Accuracy, %	99.4

The r^2 for the votes cast from 1972 to 2000 is calculated to be .9970.

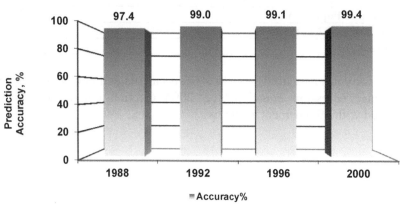

Figure 8-1 Accuracy of Democratic Regression Projections, % (1988 to 2000)

That being said, reviewing all of the predictions, a conclusion is easily made. Accurate projections of the popular vote for the Democratic candidates in 1988 through 2000 could have been determined prior to the election itself. Figure 8-1 presents a graph of the accuracies of the predictions using the results of the previous elections since 1972 (excluding 1976).

However, if the accuracy of the projections for the Republican candidates is graphed, it would not come close to those of the Democratic candidates (see Fig. 8-2). Only the projection for the 1988 election comes close to the Democratic side's accuracy with 91.9 percent accuracy.

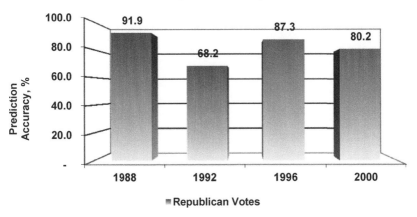

**Accuracy of Republican Regression Projections, %
(1988 to 2000)**

Figure 8-2 Accuracy of Republican Regression Predictions, %
(1988 to 2000)

A quick review of the Independent candidates yields accuracies less than 56 percent. Both of these additional projections give credibility that the presidential trend is unique and unusual.

Projecting the Popular Vote

Chapter 9

Analyzing the Baseline Trends

Introduction

As discussed in Chap. 6, the elections of 1948, 1968, and 1992 form the *baseline* or *upper limit* trends for the Republican and non-majority party candidates' voters, respectively. Subsequent analysis, as Chap. 6 reveals, the Democratic baseline dipped in 1972 to form a new baseline. Therefore, this chapter reviews the linearity and accuracy of the Republican and Independent baseline/upper limit trends then the new shifted baseline trend for the Democratic candidates.

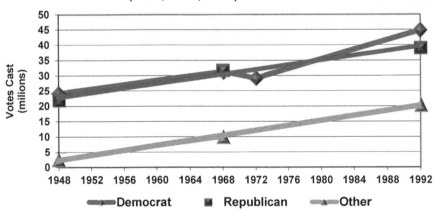

**Democratic/Republican/Independet Popular Vote
(1948, 1968, 1992) Plus Dem. 1972**

Sources: US Census Bureau Statistical Abstracts 1951 to 2004 and uselectionatlas.org

Figure 9-1 Democratic, Republican & Independent Popular Vote
(1948, 1968, 1992 plus Dem 1972)

Defining the Baseline/Upper Limit

Since the Democratic baseline shifted in 1972, only the Republican and Independent baselines are reviewed from 1948 to 1992. Therefore, regression equations are developed for the Republican and Independent baselines. Using the Republican and Independent votes cast for the election years of 1948, 1968, 1992, the following equations can be derived[90]:

$$PV_R = 0.3862x - 730$$

$$PV_I = 0.4050x - 787$$

where PV is the popular rote for R (Republican) and I (Independent) and x is the election year.

Using the above equation and substituting the appropriate year, estimates of the votes cast are calculated. Table 9-1 displays the results of accuracy of the regression equation for each baseline/upper limit.

Table 9-1 Accuracy of the Regression Equation 1948, 1968, 1992			
	1948	**1968**	**1992**
Republican, %	96.8	95.6	98.5
Independent, %	91.6	96.4	99.2

Note: Values are rounded to the nearest single decimal point. For actual values used in the calculations, see Appendix B.

Source: US Census Bureau Statistical Abstracts 1951 to 2004; the presidential trend calculations

Measuring the Linearity

A second method of determining the linearity of the 1948, 1968, and 1992 popular votes is to determine the r^2 for each baseline. The r^2 is calculated for the Republican and Independent's popular votes from

---

[90] A non-Democrat equation can be developed by adding the Republican and other candidates' equations together to get the non-Democrats popular vote = $.7912x - 1516.1$.

1948, 1968, and 1992 to reveal the degree of correlation of the election data. Table 9-2 displays the results of each.

Table 9-2 r^2 Presidential Candidates 1948, 1968, 1992	
	r^2
Republican	.9817
Independent	.9987
Democratic	.9837

Sources: US Census Bureau Statistical Abstracts 1951 to 2004; the presidential trend calculations

As Table 9-2 indicates, each of the party's r^2 shows a strong relationship. The strong relationship of these two elections for these two electoral parties represents one thing: each of these baselines/upper limit trend represents a continuation of similar voters voting from one election to another with only an increase in voting population.

Democratic Baseline Shift in 1972

As discussed in Chap. 6, there was a change in the Democrat baseline trend in 1972. The Democrat baseline dips lower from 1968 to 1972 and thus now follows the presidential trend line from 1972 to 2000. To illustrate, Fig. 9-2 shows that from 1968 to 1972 the presidential trend dips downward. This changes the path of the baseline trend. After the shift in 1972, the Democratic baseline coincides with the existing presidential trend.

Proof of the alignment of the new shifted trend with the presidential trend can be seen upon reviewing the regression formula for the line from 1972 to 1992. Usually, at least three data points are needed to develop a formula for a trend line. However, to verify the alignment of the new two points (1972 and 1992) matches the presidential trend, the accuracy of the shifted line is determined. Using only the 1972 and 1992 popular vote for the Democratic candidates, the following formula is derived:

$$PV_D = 0.4743x - 901$$

Where PV is the popular vote and x is the election year.

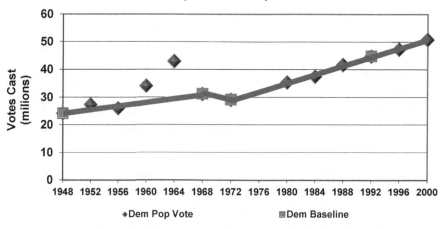

Sources: US Census Bureau Statistical Abstracts 1951 to 2004 and uselectionatlas.org

Figure 9-2 Democratic Popular Vote/Baseline w/Shift
(1948 to 2000)

Table 9-3 depicts the estimates derived from the two-point equation as well as the accuracy

Table 9-3 Popular Vote for Democratic Candidate in Presidential Elections and 1972 and 1992 Predicted Amount, 1972 to 2000 (millions)

	1972	1980	1984	1988	1992	1996	2000
Democrat	29.2	35.5	37.6	41.8	44.9	47.4	51.0
Estimate (1972 & 1992)	29.2	35.1	38.6	41.8	44.9	48.1	51.2
Accuracy, %	100.00	99.97	97.24	99.89	100.00	98.61	99.61

Sources: US Census Bureau Statistical Abstracts 1951 to 2004 and uselectionatlas.org

As shown in the table, the estimates are extremely high. Although the two baseline points (1972 and 1992) are naturally positioned at 100 percent, the accuracy of the other election years is no less than 97.24 percent. The reason for this high accuracy is that, after 1972, the Democratic votes cast are aligned with the Democratic baseline. *In essence, the two are one in the same.*

Accuracy of the two-point baseline equation is impressive. What may be even more impressive is that the votes cast for the Democratic and Republican candidates from 1948 to 2000 do not go below their baseline trends, thereby continuing to validate the existence of a core or base group of voters who always vote for a particular candidate.

Analyzing the Baseline Trends

PART 3

The State & Local Trends

Chapter 10

Analyzing the Trend State by State

Introduction

Intuitively, it stands to reason that if the national popular vote for the Democratic candidate increased in a predictable trend from 1972 to 2000 (excluding 1976), then this pattern should have existed in one or more states.[91] It is obvious that voters who made up the Democratic and non-Democratic electorates moved from state to state but did not affect the national presidential trend. However, it is also assumed that not enough population movement occurred to *not* mimic the trend at the state level.

Therefore, a likely scenario is that there existed a significant amount of states that contained a similar trend to the one displayed nationally.[92] This chapter reviews and analyzes the trend at the state level.

Predictable Trend at the State Level

Several voting-related obstacles for the trend existed at the state level, which did not completely exist at the national level. First, the population increase of the state was less stable than the population increase at the national level. That is to say, individuals moved from state to state but usually stayed inside the country. Second, the old axiom by former Speaker of the House Tip O'Neil is true: "All politics is local."

---

[91] The trend or pattern should also manifest itself at the lower levels as well.

[92] In fact, using the elections of 1972 to 2000 (excluding the 1976 election), 57 percent of the country's votes resided in states with a Democratic r^2 of greater than .80.

At the state level, voter turnout varied along with different state referendum issues and campaigns. For example, controversial state referendums most likely increased the turnout for a particular state. The combination of these two factors should have yielded a condition where the presidential trend would not be as consistent at the state level than at the national level. Consequently, in some ways the existence of the presidential trend at the state level is much more impressive than the existence at the national level.

Nonetheless, verifying the presidential trend is achieved using the same techniques used at the national level. Thus, determining the linearity of the popular vote using r^2 is the first step in verifying a predictable trend. Table 10-1 displays the states' r^2 for the popular vote of the Democratic candidate for the elections from 1972 to 2000 (excluding 1976).

It is important to mention that an r^2 greater than .8 shows a high linear correlation. As Table 10-1 indicates, 29 states have an r^2 greater than .80. Only six (6) states, including the District of Columbia, have an r^2 of less than .50.

Alternately, Table 10-2 presents the r^2 for the Republican candidates for the election of 1972 to 2000. Table 10-2 shows that there were *no* states, including the District of Columbia, that have an r^2 above .80. Furthermore, there are 39 states with an r^2 under .50. This equates to almost seven (7) times the amount of the presidential trend.

Table 10-1 State r^2 for Democratic Popular Vote, 1972 to 2000[93]

State	r^2	State	r^2
Ohio	0.989287	South Carolina	0.831398
Virginia	0.978537	Wisconsin	0.816731
Washington	0.975085	Rhode Island	0.803989
Vermont	0.971425	Tennessee	0.798299
Oregon	0.965311	Delaware	0.785447
Florida	0.963879	Indiana	0.782846
Maryland	0.962470	Georgia	0.780668
New Mexico	0.961477	Oklahoma	0.780180
Arizona	0.957177	Utah	0.766196
Maine	0.955289	Idaho	0.755245
Colorado	0.931039	Louisiana	0.746700
Hawaii	0.917098	Kansas	0.728898
North Carolina	0.914512	Alabama	0.675769
New Jersey	0.909191	Kentucky	0.656417
Illinois	0.900844	Arkansas	0.638433
Alaska	0.885900	Wyoming	0.631578
Nevada	0.882608	Iowa	0.591585
Texas	0.862737	Nebraska	0.583362
Michigan	0.860994	Massachusetts	0.512631
Connecticut	0.858940	Mississippi	0.485369
Missouri	0.858492	D.C.	0.439375
New Hampshire	0.857031	Montana	0.369761
California	0.854693	North Dakota	0.029898
Pennsylvania	0.849845	West Virginia	0.003253
Minnesota	0.848008	South Dakota	0.000223
New York	0.832146		

Sources: US Census Bureau Statistical Abstracts 1974 to 2004 and Dave Leip's *Atlas of US Presidential Elections* (uselectionatlas.org)

---

[93] Excluding the election of 1976.

State	r^2		State	r^2
Table 10-2 State r^2 for Republican Popular Vote 1972 to 2000[94]				
D.C.	0.770290		Michigan	0.192351
New York	0.741230		Idaho	0.184106
Nevada	0.731648		Oklahoma	0.177913
Alaska	0.673306		Oregon	0.138167
Illinois	0.660368		California	0.135575
Rhode Island	0.650837		Missouri	0.115496
Arizona	0.617303		Utah	0.110502
South Carolina	0.609121		Delaware	0.101279
New Jersey	0.588893		Wyoming	0.076166
Georgia	0.572575		Washington	0.073192
West Virginia	0.562190		Kentucky	0.071132
Connecticut	0.553205		Arkansas	0.070061
North Carolina	0.486951		Nebraska	0.066402
Pennsylvania	0.468120		Vermont	0.065208
Virginia	0.435583		South Dakota	0.051136
Iowa	0.426133		Kansas	0.047397
Indiana	0.413041		Louisiana	0.045034
Alabama	0.411781		Maryland	0.042440
Massachusetts	0.401788		Maine	0.032309
Florida	0.390473		New Hampshire	0.028077
Texas	0.337080		Mississippi	0.017713
Tennessee	0.326452		New Mexico	0.008066
Hawaii	0.301395		Montana	0.006651
North Dakota	0.262284		Minnesota	0.006134
Colorado	0.220204		Wisconsin	0.000529
Ohio	0.198169			

Sources: US Census Bureau Statistical Abstracts 1974 to 2004 and Dave Leip's *Atlas of US Presidential Elections* (uselectionatlas.org).

---

[94] Excluding the election of 1976.

Ohio and Virginia: Mini Presidential Trends

At the top of the states are Ohio and Virginia, which show the highest similarity with the popular vote for the national presidential trend.[95] With an r^2 of approximately .9893 and 9785, Ohio and Virginia (respectively) seem to nearly mimic the national trend. The value nationally is .976 (see Chap. 7). Below outlines the same process, statistics, and formulas used to analyze the national trend.

For the elections, from 1972 to 2000, the trend line estimated for Ohio possesses accuracies greater than 98 percent. Virginia has only one election lower than 98 percent (1980). Tables 10-3 and 10-4 clearly show that the 1972 to 2000 trends closely approximated the actual popular vote for the nation.

Table 10-3 Ohio Popular Vote for the Democratic Candidate,
1972 to 2000
(millions)

	1972	1980	1984	1988	1992	1996	2000
Democrat	1.56	1.75	1.83	1.94	1.98	2.15	2.19
Estimate	1.56	1.74	1.84	1.93	2.02	2.11	2.20
Accuracy, %	99.9	99.5	99.5	99.3	98.4	98.2	99.3

Sources: US Census Bureau Statistical Abstracts 1951 to 2002 and uselectionatlas.org

Table 10-4 Virginia Popular Vote for the Democratic Candidate,
1972 to 2000
(millions)

	1972	1980	1984	1988	1992	1996	2000
Democrat	0.44	0.75	0.80	0.86	1.04	1.09	1.22
Estimate	0.45	0.68	0.80	0.91	1.03	1.14	1.26
Accuracy, %	97.4	90.6	99.9	93.8	99.0	95.1	96.5

Sources: US Census Bureau Statistical Abstracts 1951 to 2002 and uselectionatlas.org

When the state's votes cast for the Democratic candidate for Ohio and Virginia are plotted, the graphs appear to be similar to those of the national trend (see Figs. 10-1 and 10-2).

---

[95] Using the elections of 1972 through 2004 (excluding 1976).

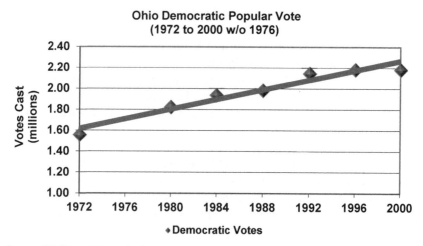

Sources: US Census Bureau Statistical Abstracts 1951 to 2002 and uselectionatlas.org

Figure 10-1 Ohio Democratic Popular Vote
(1972 to 2000 w/o 1976)

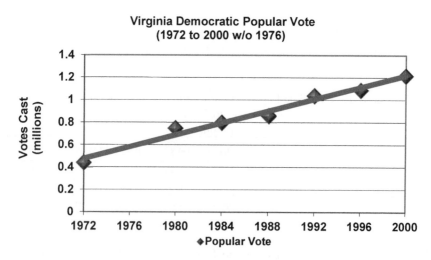

Sources: US Census Bureau Statistical Abstracts 1951 to 2002 and uselectionatlas.org

Figure 10-2 Virginia Democratic Popular Vote
(1972 to 2000 w/o 1976)

Ohio and Virginia: The Mirror Effect

As presented in Chap. 4, the fracturing of the electorate that began in 1968 and completed in 1972 caused a unique mirror effect between the Republican and non-majority party candidates' popular votes. If the presidential trend existed at the state level, there must have been a similar mirroring for the states as well. This turns out to be true.

As with the presidential trend, Ohio and Virginia possess clear examples of the mirror effect between Republican and Independent candidates. Figures 10-3 and 10-4 present the Republican as well as the Independent candidates' popular vote for the elections from 1972 to 2000 (excluding 1976). Similar to Fig. 4-2 in Chap. 4, the Republican votes cast decreased when the Independent candidates performed well. Conversely, the Independent candidates votes cast decreased when the Republican performed well. The net effect is a mirror image.

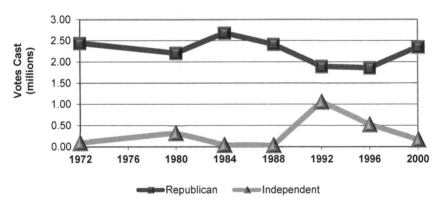

**Ohio Republican & Independent Popular Vote
(1972 to 2000 w/o 1976)**

Sources: US Census Bureau Statistical Abstracts 1951 to 2002 and uselectionatlas.org

Figure 10-3 Ohio Republican & Independent Popular Vote
(1972 to 2000 w/o 1976)

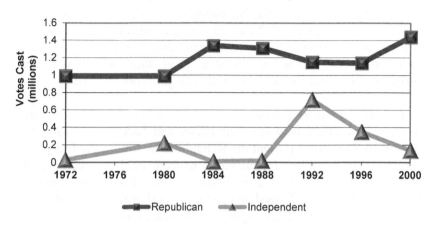

Sources: US Census Bureau Statistical Abstracts 1951 to 2002 and uselectionatlas.org

Figure 10-4 Virginia Republican & Independent Popular Vote
(1972 to 2000 w/o 1976)

It turns out that the mirror image for Ohio and Virginia is just as symmetrical as the one depicted at the national level. The linear nature of the presidential trend and the mirror effect show that fracturing had occurred not only at the national level, but also at the state level as well.

Ohio and Virginia: Baselines Trends

If the baseline elections for Ohio and Virginia are plotted for the 1948, 1968, and 1992 elections, the chart results are similar to the graphs at the national level. The plotted baseline elections show that the elections are aligned along a straight line.

As with the Democratic baseline at the national level, there is a bending upward from 1968 to 1992. To reiterate, the bending is the minor *breaking off* of Democratic base voters in 1972, which establishes a slightly different baseline that contains less Democratic voters. This seems to be the case for Virginia and to a lesser extent for Ohio.

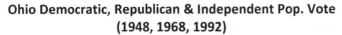

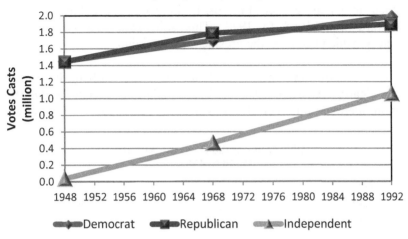

Sources: US Census Bureau Statistical Abstracts 1951 to 2002 and uselectionatlas.org

Figure 10-5 Ohio Democratic, Republican & Independent Popular Vote
(1948, 1968, 1992)

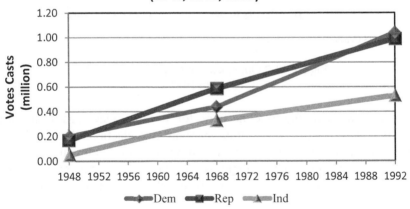

Sources: US Census Bureau Statistical Abstracts 1951 to 2002 and uselectionatlas.org

Figure 10-6 Virginia Democratic, Republican & Independent Popular Vote
(1948, 1968, 1992)

After viewing the baseline, there is one other graph to be analyzed. This graph shows the baseline shift for the Democratic candidates. As outlined in Chap. 6 (see Fig. 6-5), the Democratic baseline shifts downward from 1968 to 1972. This shift creates a new baseline trajectory, which becomes the presidential trend line.

Figure 10-7 shows the baseline shift for Ohio. The shift in the baseline can be clearly seen from 1968 to 1972. In addition, except for the 1956 election, there are no other elections that dip below the baseline, new or old.

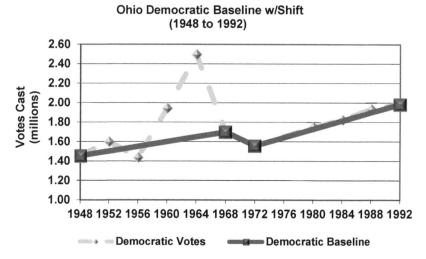

Ohio Democratic Baseline w/Shift
(1948 to 1992)

Sources: US Census Bureau Statistical Abstracts 1951 to 2002 and uselectionatlas.org

Figure 10-7 Ohio Democratic Baseline w/Shift
(1948 to 1992)

Figure 10-8 shows the baseline trend for Virginia. Once again, the shift can be clearly seen. For Virginia, there are two elections that dip below the baseline, 1956 and 1988. Even with two elections below the baseline, it is apparent that for a majority of elections, votes cast for the Democratic candidate do not cross below the amount predicted for the base.

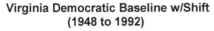

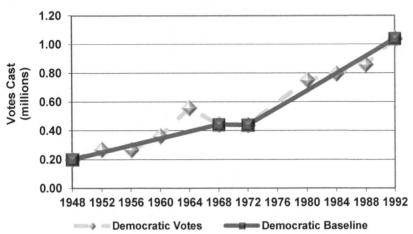

Sources: US Census Bureau Statistical Abstracts 1951 to 2002 and uselectionatlas.org

Figure 10-8 Virginia Democratic Baseline w/Shift
(1948 to 1992)

The baseline for Ohio and Virginia undoubtedly shows that the attributes of the national trend are also reflected at the state level.

The Trend of the States

The next several pages present a brief snapshot of all US states sorted by their r^2 amount for the Democratic candidate (see Tables 5 and 6). Included for each state are the following: r^2 value for the Democratic and Republican candidates; regression equation to estimate the popular vote for the Democratic candidate (in millions); and a table listing the vote for the Democratic candidate for the elections of 1972 to 2000 (excluding 1976) plus the accuracy of the regression equation from the trend line.

The accuracy developed is determined by comparing the r^2 trend line estimate to the actual vote. Estimated elections that are leas than 90 percent accurate are shaded.

Table 10-5 States' Accuracy of 1972 to 2000 Presidential Trend Line
(Sorted by States' r^2)

State	R^2	1972	1980	1984	1988	1992	1996	2000
Ohio	0.9893	99.9	99.5	99.5	99.3	98.3	98.2	97.3
Virginia	0.9785	91.7	91.4	99.7	95.3	96.9	98.0	96.3
Washington	0.9751	90.7	89.8	98.8	98.3	97.5	99.6	99.7
Vermont	0.9714	93.1	91.9	94.5	98.0	94.3	99.5	100.0
Oregon	0.9653	99.3	94.1	98.9	93.7	99.6	96.7	97.0
Florida	0.9639	91.3	88.9	92.0	87.2	95.2	97.2	99.8
Maryland	0.9625	96.5	95.4	98.6	95.7	95.7	93.3	98.5
New Mexico	0.9615	97.5	90.9	98.0	93.5	96.0	99.8	99.0
Arizona	0.9572	72.0	78.6	86.8	99.5	98.4	93.8	98.4
Maine	0.9553	99.4	93.0	93.6	96.8	95.9	95.0	97.3
Colorado	0.9310	90.6	84.1	92.3	89.1	98.1	98.5	99.5
Hawaii	0.9171	95.4	98.8	95.9	87.8	97.1	97.7	94.5
North Carolina	0.9145	81.4	83.7	98.2	93.8	94.4	95.5	95.4
New Jersey	0.9092	90.4	95.5	96.9	93.9	95.4	97.1	98.3
Illinois	0.9008	96.5	96.9	97.4	98.9	95.3	96.0	98.5
Alaska	0.8859	94.3	80.8	92.6	89.5	92.6	99.5	95.9
Nevada	0.8826	39.4	66.8	68.8	85.7	96.8	94.8	98.8
Texas	0.8627	80.3	92.5	98.5	89.2	99.8	99.9	98.0
Michigan	0.8610	94.9	95.2	90.1	93.8	99.6	99.3	99.4
Connecticut	0.8589	90.2	92.9	91.2	97.5	97.5	99.6	98.0
Missouri	0.8585	93.5	91.5	93.2	95.9	96.3	95.8	99.5
New Hampshire	0.8570	68.1	81.2	71.8	90.4	97.8	93.2	98.1
California	0.8547	85.9	78.2	94.5	96.2	95.9	96.6	98.2
Pennsylvania	0.8498	98.4	96.9	93.5	98.8	99.3	94.3	99.2
Minnesota	0.8480	94.2	98.8	95.5	93.5	93.8	99.0	97.9
New York	0.8321	90.1	89.4	97.5	99.1	96.8	99.4	98.8
South Carolina	0.8314	78.4	75.8	92.2	87.1	97.1	98.3	96.9
Wisconsin	0.8167	95.7	96.3	100.0	92.8	94.7	93.1	99.2
Rhode Island	0.8040	95.5	98.5	93.9	96.4	94.6	99.8	98.2
Tennessee	0.7983	71.2	79.0	98.0	85.8	91.6	97.2	99.9
Delaware	0.7854	85.9	96.0	89.2	86.1	93.1	96.1	96.7
Indiana	0.7828	93.8	94.6	97.7	98.2	97.7	99.5	93.8
Georgia	0.7807	54.1	70.9	95.8	82.4	93.7	99.6	96.6
Oklahoma	0.7802	79.3	90.1	97.6	88.2	96.9	99.5	98.9
Trend line	0.7662	94.2	81.1	95.6	85.1	95.9	92.6	96.0
Idaho	0.7552	92.1	97.8	91.2	87.1	98.8	90.0	98.5
Louisiana	0.7467	57.0	80.3	98.3	99.2	96.0	92.1	98.6
Kansas	0.7289	93.3	100.0	96.4	86.1	98.1	96.3	98.2
Alabama	0.6758	53.8	75.4	96.5	93.5	92.4	95.8	97.1
Kentucky	0.6564	79.3	83.7	98.2	99.5	92.7	97.8	99.1
Arkansas	0.6384	72.4	80.7	95.1	88.6	83.6	96.1	96.3
Wyoming	0.6316	98.4	93.0	93.6	90.4	94.7	87.9	99.5
Iowa	0.5916	97.4	91.7	94.4	88.3	95.4	97.8	99.6
Nebraska	0.5834	97.9	86.7	93.4	81.5	97.4	99.0	95.9

Table 10-5 States' Accuracy of 1972 to 2000 Presidential Trend Line (Sorted by States' r^2)

Massachusetts	0.5126	85.6	80.8	94.1	97.8	91.7	94.5	99.1
Mississippi	0.4854	12.2	69.4	93.0	98.2	96.7	94.2	98.2
DC	0.4394	94.8	86.6	85.5	99.0	87.1	89.8	98.9
Montana	0.3698	96.4	85.6	95.6	86.1	97.6	92.9	97.3
North Dakota	0.0299	97.5	73.8	96.7	79.9	96.1	97.4	97.4
West Virginia	0.0033	84.2	87.8	98.6	95.1	98.1	99.3	97.0
South Dakota	0.0002	90.4	78.0	90.8	87.2	98.3	91.2	98.8
Percent >90%		64.7	49.0	90.2	60.8	96.1	94.1	100.0

Sources: US Census Bureau Statistical Abstracts 1951 to 2002 and uselectionatlas.org

Table 10-6 States' Accuracy of 1972 to 2000 Republican Trend Line (Sorted by States' r^2)

State	R^2	1972	1980	1984	1988	1992	1996	2000
District of Columbia	0.77029	95.4	76.2	91.3	87.4	94.9	88.2	93.5
New York	0.74123	96.0	80.5	86.6	93.8	88.9	79.8	94.7
Nevada	0.73165	97.9	99.3	92.3	94.5	77.7	81.9	93.2
Alaska	0.67331	81.9	95.4	74.0	96.3	75.3	86.3	98.0
Illinois	0.66037	99.1	93.9	86.7	94.9	82.5	81.3	94.7
Rhode Island	0.65084	98.9	78.0	82.1	89.8	89.8	75.4	94.6
Arizona	0.61730	86.8	98.5	84.9	88.1	84.7	87.4	95.8
South Carolina	0.60912	92.8	83.1	89.7	96.9	92.0	84.9	98.8
New Jersey	0.58889	95.6	88.2	84.3	87.8	94.5	79.2	94.3
Georgia	0.57258	84.5	63.8	90.2	95.8	88.6	90.6	95.8
West Virginia	0.56219	91.0	84.4	88.5	93.1	74.4	81.9	94.4
Connecticut	0.55321	94.7	87.3	80.6	89.6	91.6	79.6	94.1
North Carolina	0.48695	91.5	80.0	86.5	99.4	85.8	88.9	98.3
Pennsylvania	0.46812	97.0	92.4	90.3	97.1	80.9	87.1	95.2
Virginia	0.43558	97.9	88.4	86.2	91.6	91.6	86.2	96.9
Iowa	0.42613	100.0	97.0	89.7	89.0	85.1	87.3	95.1
Indiana	0.41304	99.4	95.9	91.7	93.9	81.3	87.7	95.1
Alabama	0.41178	96.2	85.1	89.0	98.3	2.7	89.2	97.5
Massachusetts	0.40179	89.3	94.4	80.8	83.9	82.5	76.2	97.1
Florida	0.39047	93.4	93.4	83.6	91.0	85.7	84.8	94.4
Texas	0.33708	96.0	94.2	81.2	96.2	77.7	83.6	96.6
Tennessee	0.32645	99.4	91.3	88.9	95.5	89.7	89.7	96.4
Hawaii	0.30140	100.0	78.8	82.2	92.4	97.0	81.2	84.3

Table 10-6 States' Accuracy of 1972 to 2000 Republican Trend Line
(Sorted by States' r^2)

North Dakota	0.26228	90.8	92.0	86.0	99.9	82.2	76.4	95.3
Colorado	0.22020	96.5	98.3	83.5	97.3	70.1	91.0	95.4
Ohio	0.19817	98.5	92.7	86.3	93.4	83.8	84.6	95.1
Michigan	0.19235	95.2	97.7	84.8	94.7	83.3	80.8	94.7
Idaho	0.18411	85.7	84.6	85.7	96.1	65.4	90.2	96.1
Oklahoma	0.17791	98.8	94.5	83.2	96.9	84.9	85.7	95.2
Oregon	0.13817	92.9	96.2	82.2	96.8	75.6	87.3	93.4
California	0.13558	93.5	96.0	84.3	89.2	78.4	87.3	94.7
Missouri	0.11550	99.7	96.5	85.4	98.2	71.6	85.6	96.1
Utah	0.11050	86.0	88.6	85.2	95.7	69.7	81.0	93.0
Delaware	0.10128	97.5	82.0	84.4	90.0	80.0	78.9	93.5
Washington	0.07319	98.6	98.5	84.9	99.6	73.9	88.5	95.9
Kentucky	0.07113	98.8	91.3	85.3	97.1	82.6	81.9	95.8
Arkansas	0.07006	97.1	90.4	81.1	91.2	76.4	74.4	98.8
Nebraska	0.06640	96.6	98.0	88.6	98.8	84.2	91.4	94.7
Vermont	0.06521	100.0	80.9	81.3	87.1	79.6	70.7	96.7
South Dakota	0.05114	91.0	89.2	87.2	95.8	75.7	88.6	93.8
Kansas	0.04740	97.9	95.2	86.7	95.1	72.3	97.4	96.0
Louisiana	0.04503	86.3	98.6	78.6	93.5	85.7	80.8	97.7
Maryland	0.04244	97.7	83.1	89.5	89.0	90.8	87.8	94.4
Maine	0.03231	92.7	88.0	78.2	84.4	76.5	65.3	95.4
New Hampshire	0.02808	93.8	95.4	87.8	84.2	81.7	76.8	95.6
Mississippi	0.01771	98.9	85.2	87.6	91.9	94.2	81.9	97.9
New Mexico	0.00807	93.1	98.6	83.2	95.0	78.8	88.6	93.0
Montana	0.00665	95.4	94.2	84.3	96.6	62.6	89.1	96.7
Minnesota	0.00613	99.8	96.4	88.1	94.9	77.3	79.7	95.4
Wisconsin	0.00053	94.6	96.0	87.3	99.9	87.2	75.6	93.8
Wyoming	0.07617	98.4	96.9	82.4	94.9	55.2	88.5	97.5
Percent >90%		86.3	60.8	9.8	74.5	15.7	9.8	98.0

Sources: US Census Bureau Statistical Abstracts 1951 to 2002 and uselectionatlas.org

States with Low Trend Linearity

A detailed review of the state statistics that possess a low Democratic r^2 (or trend correlation) reveals that many have decreased or relatively unchanged votes casts for the Democratic candidate. Consequently, the presidential trend may have still existed in a particular state but was masked due to an inconsistent increase in population. That is to say that the electorate could have been fractured, but a non-increasing population failed to make the trend visible. Therefore, the decreasing or unchanging population may have created lower r^2 values for the states. To study this further, review Table 10-7, which present each state's population change from 1970 to 2000 in addition to each state's Democratic and Republican r^2 amount.

Table 10-7 State Population Change, 1970 to 2000
Sorted by State Population Change
(million)

NAME	DEM7200 r^2	REP7200 r^2	POP 1970	POP 2000	Chg. %
Nevada	0.8826	0.73165	0.55	2.00	265.5
Arizona	0.9572	0.61730	2.01	5.13	155.4
Florida	0.9639	0.39047	7.52	15.98	112.5
Utah	0.7662	0.11050	1.13	2.23	96.8
Alaska	0.8859	0.67331	0.33	0.63	92.0
Colorado	0.9310	0.22020	2.40	4.30	78.9
Texas	0.8627	0.33708	11.76	20.85	77.3
Washington	0.9751	0.07319	3.45	5.89	71.0
Georgia	0.7807	0.57258	4.81	8.19	70.3
Idaho	0.7552	0.18411	0.76	1.29	69.5
New Mexico	0.9615	0.00807	1.08	1.82	68.8
California	0.8547	0.13558	20.58	33.87	64.5
New Hampshire	0.8570	0.02808	0.78	1.24	58.1
Oregon	0.9653	0.13817	2.20	3.42	55.9
North Carolina	0.9145	0.48695	5.30	8.05	52.0
South Carolina	0.8314	0.60912	2.72	4.01	47.6
Virginia	0.9785	0.43558	4.83	7.08	46.6
Hawaii	0.9171	0.30140	0.83	1.21	46.4
Wyoming	0.6316	0.07617	0.35	0.49	42.4
Tennessee	0.7983	0.32645	4.09	5.69	39.2
Delaware	0.7854	0.10128	0.57	0.78	36.6

Table 10-7 State Population Change, 1970 to 2000
Sorted by State Population Change
(million)

NAME	DEM7200 r^2	REP7200 r^2	POP 1970	POP 2000	Chg. %
Arkansas	0.6384	0.07006	2.02	2.67	32.5
Vermont	0.9714	0.06521	0.46	0.61	31.4
Maryland	0.9625	0.04244	4.08	5.30	29.8
Oklahoma	0.7802	0.17791	2.66	3.45	29.8
Minnesota	0.8480	0.00613	3.87	4.92	27.2
Alabama	0.6758	0.41178	3.54	4.45	25.6
Montana	0.3698	0.00665	0.72	0.90	25.5
Mississippi	0.4854	0.01771	2.31	2.84	23.3
Maine	0.9553	0.03231	1.03	1.27	23.2
Kentucky	0.6564	0.07113	3.34	4.04	21.2
Kansas	0.7289	0.04740	2.26	2.69	19.2
Wisconsin	0.8167	0.00053	4.50	5.36	19.2
Louisiana	0.7467	0.04503	3.76	4.47	18.8
Missouri	0.8585	0.11550	4.75	5.60	17.7
Indiana	0.7828	0.41304	5.30	6.08	14.8
New Jersey	0.9092	0.58889	7.34	8.41	14.7
Nebraska	0.5834	0.06640	1.52	1.71	12.7
South Dakota	0.0002	0.05114	0.68	0.75	11.4
Connecticut	0.8589	0.55321	3.07	3.41	10.9
Illinois	0.9008	0.66037	11.26	12.42	10.3
Massachusetts	0.5126	0.40179	5.76	6.35	10.2
Michigan	0.8610	0.19235	9.02	9.94	10.1
Rhode Island	0.8040	0.65084	0.98	1.05	7.4
Ohio	0.9893	0.19817	10.75	11.35	5.6
New York	0.8321	0.74123	18.35	18.98	3.4
Pennsylvania	0.8498	0.46812	11.90	12.28	3.2
Iowa	0.5916	0.42613	2.86	2.93	2.3
North Dakota	0.0299	0.26228	0.63	0.64	1.8
West Virginia	0.0033	0.56219	1.80	1.81	0.6
District of Columbia	0.4394	0.77029	0.74	0.57	-23.1

Source: US Census Bureau, *Demographic Trends in the 20th Century*, 2002 (Table #1)

At first glance, Table 10-7 may not readily reveal that the states with the lowest population change also have the lowest r^2.[96] However, if the states are grouped together by their increase in population, the effect on the r^2 value come to light. For instance, Fig. 10-9 shows a graph with the states grouped into three ranges of population increase: 1) less than 25 percent; 2) 25 to 100 percent; and 3) greater than 100 percent.

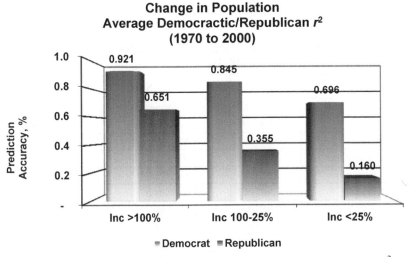

Figure 10-9 Change in Population, Average Democrat/Republican r^2
(1970 to 2000)

However, the states with a population increase of 25 to 100 percent have an average Democratic r^2 value of .845 with the Republican r^2 value of .355. The states with the highest population increase, which is greater than 100 percent, have a Democratic and Republican r^2 of .921 and .651, respectively. In each case, the decreasing population change yields a decrease in the r^2 value. This validates the possibility that the decreasing population throughout the states could be causing some of the low r^2 values

---

[96] The national population increased from 203.2 million in 1970 to 281.4 million in 2000 with an increase of 38.5 percent (*Source*: US Census Bureau, Decennial Census Population, 1900 to 2000)

Baseline Trends for the States

If the states show a trend for the Democratic candidates from 1972 to 2000, it stands to reason that there would also be a baseline trend for the years, 1948, 1968, and 1992. Below lists the states' baseline trend for the Democratic, Republican and Independent party candidates. As stated previously, the Democratic baseline shifts in 1968 and 1972 to form a new trend. Nonetheless, the Democratic candidates table is included.

Table 10-8 States' r^2 for Democratic Candidates for President, 1948, 1968, 1992

State	r^2		State	r^2
Ohio	0.999487		Arizona	0.904549
California	0.997591		New Mexico	0.898332
Minnesota	0.996633		Connecticut	0.882227
South Carolina	0.989558		Tennessee	0.876120
Delaware	0.989119		Georgia	0.865729
Maryland	0.987747		Arkansas	0.861266
West Virginia	0.984706		Illinois	0.860857
Mississippi	0.984100		South Dakota	0.834221
Oregon	0.971735		North Carolina	0.799069
Texas	0.970865		New York	0.781749
Virginia	0.965014		Indiana	0.773967
Alabama	0.963614		Montana	0.695571
Vermont	0.961821		Pennsylvania	0.670368
Washington	0.957635		North Dakota	0.618021
Wisconsin	0.951932		Kentucky	0.562040
Louisiana	0.950626		Wyoming	0.503054
New Hampshire	0.935324		Idaho	0.429378
Michigan	0.935159		Iowa	0.387475
New Jersey	0.933831		Missouri	0.318283
Florida	0.933701		Kansas	0.236214
Utah	0.933412		Massachusetts	0.230465
Maine	0.926102		Rhode Island	0.140990
Colorado	0.915685		Oklahoma	0.025669
Nevada	0.914737		Nebraska	0.004250

Sources: US Census Bureau Statistical Abstracts 1951 to 2002 and uselectionatlas.org

Note: Alaska, Hawaii, and Washington, DC, were not included in the analysis.

Table 10-9 States' r^2 for Republican Candidates for President, 1948, 1968, 1992

State	r^2		State	r^2
Kentucky	0.999345		Oregon	0.931186
South Carolina	0.999140		Nebraska	0.918426
Virginia	0.998687		Mississippi	0.907394
Arkansas	0.998653		Wyoming	0.903115
Tennessee	0.998297		Vermont	0.898287
Texas	0.998225		Alabama	0.886810
North Carolina	0.998153		Ohio	0.879281
New Hampshire	0.997498		West Virginia	0.872990
Colorado	0.993068		Delaware	0.836438
Arizona	0.992881		Connecticut	0.823701
Maryland	0.989668		Montana	0.792945
Florida	0.985534		California	0.777465
Oklahoma	0.985466		New Jersey	0.769335
Maine	0.982540		Missouri	0.699135
Utah	0.980005		North Dakota	0.616111
Georgia	0.979901		New York	0.568919
Washington	0.976841		Massachusetts	0.447364
Nevada	0.969347		Indiana	0.393475
Louisiana	0.961538		Illinois	0.312679
Idaho	0.959099		Kansas	0.191006
Michigan	0.953645		Pennsylvania	0.171573
Wisconsin	0.953033		South Dakota	0.087522
Minnesota	0.944170		Rhode Island	0.064239
New Mexico	0.937797		Iowa	0.000681

Sources: US Census Bureau Statistical Abstracts 1951 to 2002 and uselectionatlas.org

Note: Alaska, Hawaii, and Washington, DC, were not included in the analysis.

Table 10-10 States' r^2 for Independent Candidates for President, 1948, 1968, 1992

State	r^2		State	r^2
Illinois	0.999646		Nevada	0.884795
Delaware	0.999612		Montana	0.878576
New Jersey	0.999552		Arizona	0.877285
Ohio	0.998153		Rhode Island	0.876697
Indiana	0.996535		Washington	0.868312
Missouri	0.993229		Utah	0.864466
Pennsylvania	0.991387		Oregon	0.857641
Texas	0.990157		Massachusetts	0.850235
Florida	0.989820		New Hampshire	0.847498
Michigan	0.986085		North Dakota	0.845059
Oklahoma	0.975145		Minnesota	0.840039
Maryland	0.973338		Vermont	0.836663
New Mexico	0.960623		Maine	0.806260
West Virginia	0.952786		Virginia	0.802551
Kansas	0.950604		Kentucky	0.762494
Nebraska	0.949702		New York	0.614571
Idaho	0.935679		North Carolina	0.397039
Iowa	0.927199		Georgia	0.217214
Wyoming	0.920231		South Carolina	0.106657
Wisconsin	0.912041		Tennessee	0.104457
Connecticut	0.903618		Arkansas	0.080174
Colorado	0.898928		Mississippi	0.073184
California	0.894097		Louisiana	0.001721
South Dakota	0.892040		Alabama	0.000395

Sources: US Census Bureau Statistical Abstracts 1951 to 2002 and uselectionatlas.org

Note: Alaska, Hawaii, and Washington, DC, were not included in the analysis.

Chapter 11

Mapping the State Trend

Introduction

An old Chinese proverb stated, "A picture is worth a thousand words." Thus, additional analysis of the presidential trend can be achieved using thematic maps. Thematic maps display spatial data using specific themes. In this case, each state is presented on a map with different shading depending upon its presidential trend's r^2 value. The next several pages present a series of maps that compare the population increase along with maps of the states' r^2 value. Finally, although the baseline for the Democratic candidate has been shown to *shift*, maps are still presented.

Map Analysis

As discussed in Chap. 10, the states with the lowest population increase also tend to have the lowest r^2 value. Comparing the states population change map (Fig. 11-1) to the next two maps (Figs. 11-2 and 11-3) further validate the conclusions of Chap. 10. Further analysis shows a dramatic difference between the Republican trend maps and the Republican baseline maps. Very few states show even a moderate r^2 value on the Republican trend maps while a sizable amount of states show high r^2 values on the Republican baseline maps. Finally, the non-majority party candidates' upper limit maps (Fig. 11-6) indicate a lower r^2 value in the southern states. This is in direct contrast with the high change in population in those states.[97]

---

[97] This may have been caused by the steady transition of non-majority party candidates' voters (old democrats) switching their votes to Republican candidates (inside the theoretical non-Democratic electorate).

Population Change

Figure 11-1 displays a map that depicts the state's population change from 1970 to 2000. The states with a population increase of less than 25 percent have no shading. The states with 25 to 100 percent population increase are displayed in a light shade. Those states with greater than 100 percent are displayed in a darker shade.

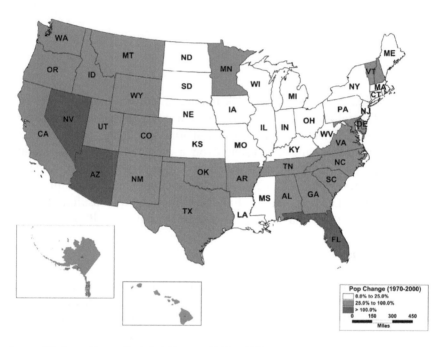

Source: US Census Bureau Statistical Abstracts 1951 to 2002

Figure 11-1 Population Change
(1970 to 2000)

Democratic Trend (The Presidential Trend) (1972 to 2000)

Figure 11-2 displays a map that depicts the r^2 value of the popular vote for the Democratic candidate for president from 1972 to 2000 (excluding 1976). The states with an r^2 of less than .70 have no shading. The states with an r^2 between .70 to .90 are displayed in a light shade. Those states with greater than .90 are displayed in a darker shade.

Source: US Census Bureau Statistical Abstracts 1951 to 2002

Figure 11-2 Democratic R-Squared
(1972 to 2000 w/o 1076)

Republican Trend (1972 to 2000)

Figure 11-3 displays a map that depicts the r^2 of the popular vote for the Republican candidate for president from 1972 to 2000 (excluding 1976). The states with an r^2 value of less than .70 have no shading. The states with an r^2 between .70 to .90 are displayed in a light shade. Those states with greater than .90 are displayed in a darker shade.

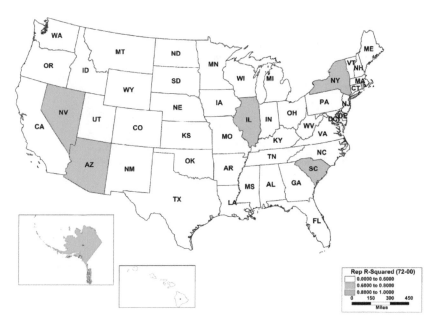

Source: US Census Bureau Statistical Abstracts 1951 to 2002

Figure 11-3 Republican r^2
(1972 to 2000 w/o 1976)

Democratic Baseline Trend (1948, 1968, 1992)

Figure 11-4 displays a map that depicts the R-Squared value of the popular vote for the Democratic candidate for president for the 1948, 1968, and 1992 elections. The states with a R-Squared value of less than .70 have no shading. The states with a R-Squared between .70 to .90 are displayed in a light shade. Those states with greater than .90 are displayed in a darker shade.

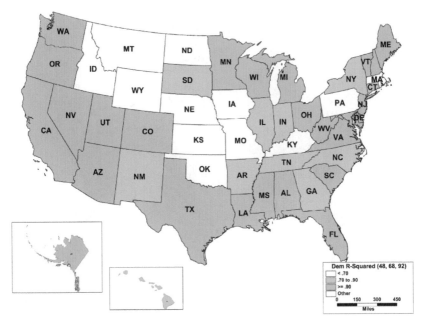

Source: U.S. Census Bureau Statistical Abstracts 1951-2002

Figure 11-4 - Democrat Baseline r^2
(1948, 1968 & 1992)

Republican Baseline Trend (1948, 1968, 1992)

Figure 11-5 displays a map that depicts the r^2 value of the popular vote for the Republican candidate for president for the 1948, 1968, and 1992 elections. The states with an r^2 value of less than .70 have no shading. The states with an r^2 between .70 to .90 are displayed in a light shade. Those states with greater than .90 are displayed in a darker shade.[98]

Source: US Census Bureau Statistical Abstracts 1951 to 2002

Figure 11-5 Republican Baseline r^2
(1948, 1968, 1992)

---

[98] Note the large amount of states with a high r^2.

Independent Upper Limit Trend (1948, 1968, 1992)

As Fig. 10-3 indicates, those states that have a population increase from, 1970 to 2000, which is less than 25 percent, have an average Democrat r^2 value of .696. The corresponding average Republican r^2 value is calculated to be .160. Figure 11-6 displays a map that depicts the r^2 value of the popular vote for the Independent candidates for president for the 1948, 1968, and 1992 elections. The states with an r^2 of less than .70 have no shading. The states with between .70 to .90 r^2 are displayed in a light shade. Those states with greater than .90 are displayed in a darker shade.[99]

Source: US Census Bureau Statistical Abstracts 1951 to 2002

Figure 11-6 Independent Upper Limit r^2
(1948, 1968, 1992)

---

[99] Note the non-shaded states in the south. After the fracturing of the electorate in 1968, there was a steady transition of other candidate voters (old Democrats) becoming Republicans.

Mapping the State Trend

Chapter 12

Analyzing the County Trend

Introduction

If the trend exists both at the national and state levels, is it possible that it exists at the county level? This chapter investigates whether the county level shows the same effects seen at the state and national level.

Predictable Trend at the County Level

The potential of the trend manifesting itself at the state level has several voting related obstacles that do not fully exist at the national level. The population increase of the state is less stable than the population increase at the national level. That is to say, individuals move from state to state but usually stay inside the country. Voter turnout varies at the state level along with different state referendum issues and campaigns. The county level has the same obstacles, except the population can potentially change at a much higher rate. This varying of population, and thus consequently voter turnout, is expected to diminish the linearity of the trend.

Since data are not readily available for a batch of counties, the first step is to plot the election results of a single county. The purpose of this analysis is to discover the trend that existed at the county level. The county initially thought of is my hometown, Hampton, Virginia. Hampton is actually an independent city, but the US Census Bureau designates it at the county level.

Once the presidential data are obtained for Hampton, they are plotted on the same scatter-plot-type graph as before. The first graph plotted is for the trend itself. Figure 12-1 displays the graph of the votes cast for the

Democratic candidates for president. As with the others the outlier election, 1976 is not included.

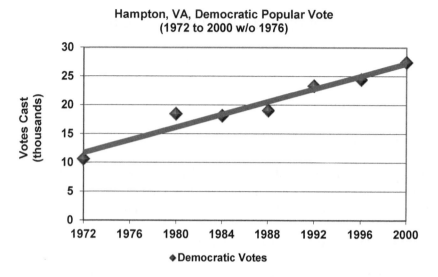

Sources: David Leip's Atlas of Presidential Elections, County data and uselectionatlas.org

Figure 12-1 Hampton, VA Democratic Popular Vote
(1972 to 2000 w/o 1976)

Although Hampton presidential trend is not as linear as the national or even most of the states, the graph clearly shows a linear pattern. In fact, the r^2 value .9467 (with a value of "1" being a straight line). The national trend is .9970 while the trend for the state of Virginia is .9785.

Verifying the accuracy proved that the trend for Hampton is fairly close in predicting votes cast for the Democratic candidate. Table 12-1 shows that the worst accuracy for the trend line is 87.2 percent while the best is 99.1 percent. The least accurate estimate occurs in 1980. Apparently, the Democratic candidate, Jimmy Carter (a southerner), was able to appeal to voters in Hampton, Virginia than he did at the national level.

Table 12-1 Hampton Democratic Popular Vote, 1972 to 2000
(thousands)

	1972	1980	1984	1988	1992	1996	2000
Democratic Votes	10.65	18.52	18.18	19.11	23.40	24.50	27.49
Estimated Votes	11.71	16.14	18.36	20.58	22.80	25.01	27.23
Accuracy, %	90.1	87.2	99.0	92.3	97.4	97.9	99.1

Sources: US Census Bureau Statistical Abstracts 1951 to 2002 and uselectionatlas.org

The next step is to analyze the secondary consequence of the fracturing of the electorate, the mirror effect. If the fracturing truly exists at the county level, the mirror effect will be prevalent as well. To reiterate, the mirror effect is displayed by the Republican and Independent candidates' votes cast mirroring each other. They mirror each other because they are, in essence, separate from the Democratic electorate in an electorate with only two types of voters.

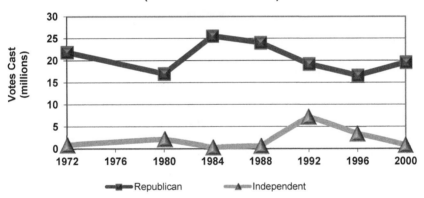

Hampton, VA, Republican & Independent Popular Vote (1972 to 2000 w/o 1976)

Sources: David Leip's Atlas of Presidential Elections, County data and uselectionatlas.org

Figure 12-2 Hampton, VA Republican & Independent Popular Vote
(1972 to 2000 w/o 1976)

Once again, the pattern is not as prevalent as those of the national and state, but nonetheless mirroring is displayed. Thus, with the trend reviewed and the mirror effect presented, there is only on last aspect of the trend theory to review: the baseline trends.

To analyze the baseline trend, data from the three baseline elections (1948, 1968, 1992) are obtained. Figure 12-3 shows the results of the baseline data for Hampton, Virginia.

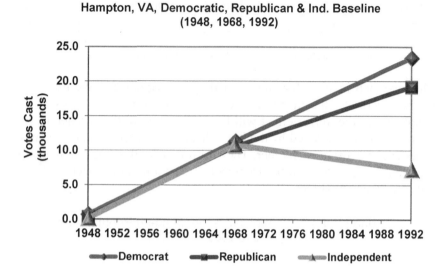

Sources: David Leip's Atlas of Presidential Elections, County data and uselectionatlas.org

Figure 12-3 Hampton, VA, Democratic, Republican & Independent Baseline (1948, 1968, 1992)

The graph clearly shows that a baseline trend existed for the Democratic and Republican candidates. However, the upper limit trend for the Independent candidates is not linear (notice the bend for the Independent candidates). The r^2 value of the Democratic and Republican trends are .9998 and .99051, respectively. The values reflect two extremely linear baselines. However, the Independent candidates' trend has an r^2 of .38132.

Once again the adage "all politics is local" holds true. For some reason, in Hampton, the Independent candidates either performed exceptional well in 1968 or did not perform well in 1992. Given the performance in 1968 of Wallace that showed him equaling the Democratic and Republican candidates, he seems to have performed exceptional well in Hampton, VA. In this city, Wallace was able to turnout additional voters that exceeded the upper-limit trend.

There is one final graph that should be developed along with one final question answered: did the baseline for the Democratic candidates show the shift in 1972 as the national trend? Figure 12-4 reveals the answer. Yes. The Democratic votes cast took a definite dip down from 1968 to 1972 (see solid line). Excluding a dip in 1988, all other votes cast remain above the baseline, as it should (see dash line).

Hampton, VA, Democratic Popular Vote/Baseline w/Shift (1948 - 1992)

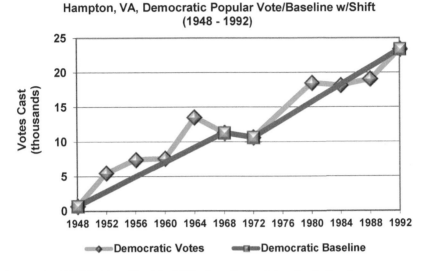

Sources: David Leip's Atlas of Presidential Elections, County data and uselectionatlas.org

Figure 12-4 Hampton, VA, Democratic Popular Vote/Baseline w/Shift (1948 - 1992)

Figure 12-4 indicates that even the shift in the Democratic baseline is replicated at the county level. The reflection of almost all aspects of the trend is reminiscent of the math phrase, "The whole is equal to the sum of its parts." This statement, when related to the trend, is also true.

At the state level, voter turnout varies along with different state referendum issues and campaigns. For example, controversial state referendums have the potential effect of increasing the turnout for a particular state. The combination of these two factors should have yielded a condition where the trend would not be as consistent at the state level than at the national level. Consequently, in some ways the very existence of the trend, at the state level, is much more impressive than the existence at the national level.

Analyzing the County Trend

PART 4

Exit Poll Trend Analysis

Chapter 13

Analysis of the Trend Using Exit Polls

Introduction

Previous chapters demonstrate that the popular vote for the Democratic candidate increased in a linear manner from 1972 to 2000, excluding 1976. This occurred mostly because the vote for the Democratic candidate consisted essentially of the previous voters who voted for the Democratic candidate plus a new batch of first-time voters. There was only a relatively smaller amount of voters that switched from non-Democratic candidates to Democratic candidates. Because of this scenario, the Democratic candidates' votes increased similarly to the increase in population.

However, political scientists and analysts tend to want to validate theories with voter surveys and polls. Therefore, it would be negligent to *not* include a chapter on exit polls. Thus, did exit polls corroborate the theory of the presidential trend? In addition, how did exit polls reflect the racial/ethnic demographic breakdown of the voters? This chapter analyzes the partisan as well as the demographic breakdown of the trend.

Trend Analysis of Exit Polls by Party Type

Using the voting results, it appears as though the voting electorate had essentially fractured into two parts. The apparent fracturing led to the popular vote results for the Democratic candidate trending in a *linear* manner from election to election until 2000 (excluding 1976).

Previously, evidence is presented that mostly Democratic voters existed in the theoretical Democratic electorate. This theory tends to be validated by the existence of the linear trend and shows that if first-time voters are added to the previous Democratic popular vote, the sum is extremely close to the actual votes cast for a given election (for the elections of 1984 to 2000). However, do exit polls indicate the same or similar results? Exit polls should reveal that a sizable amount of voters voted for the Democratic candidate and previously voted for the Democratic candidate. If the trend truly existed, exit polls should show that the popular vote for these consistent Democratic voters form an increasing linear votes cast.

Table 13-1 displays exit poll data from 1972 to 2000 for the percentage of total vote by party.[100] The data are broken down by the "party voted for" and the "previously party voted for."

Table 13-1 Vote for Pres. Candidates by Party and Previous Party, % 1984 to 2000

	1972	1980	1984	1988	1992	1996	2000
Dem Dem, %	18.5	28.3	24.8	25.9	23.9	38.5	43.8
Dem Rep, %	4.6	4.6	6.6	9.6	10.3	3.4	1.9
Dem Ind, %	2.6	0.8	3.4	1.8	1.3	2.2	2.4
Dem Not Vote	10.5%	4.8%	4.8%	6.6%	7.5%	4.8%	3.5%
Rep Dem, %	5.1	13.5	6.0	2.1	1.5	3.9	5.8
Rep Rep, %	42.6	29.6	46.9	46.7%	31.5	28.3	27.9
Rep Ind, %	3.7	1.4	1.2	0.4	0.2	5.6	5.6
Rep Not Vote	10.5%	6.3%	6.0%	5.4%	4.8%	3.5%	3.6%
Ind Dem, %	0.3	5.0	0.1	0.2	3.2	2.5	1.9
Ind Rep, %	0.4	3.2	0.2	0.6	10.8	1.4	0.8
Ind Ind, %	0.8	0.9	0.0	0.5	0.5	4.7	2.2
Ind NotVote	0.5%	1.8%	0.0%	0.3%	4.5%	1.2%	0.7%

Sources: Roper Center for Public Opinion Research National Election Day Polls (weighted samples used when available); CBS News poll, 1972, ABC News poll, 1980 to 1984; *Los Angeles Times* polls, 1988 to 2000

For example, the row "Dem Dem" provides the percentage of the total turnout who voted for the Democratic candidate for the given year and previously voted for the Democratic candidate *in the prior presidential election*. It is important to note that this considers *only* the prior election.

---

[100] Excluding 1976.

On the other hand, "Dem Rep" provides the percentage of the total turnout who voted for the Democratic candidate and previously voted for the Republican candidate.

The first aspect of the data noticed is that voters who voted for Democratic candidate and previously voted for the Democratic candidate tend to increase from election to election. However, is this increase linear? It is difficult to determine since turnout fluctuates from election to election. In order to answer this question, the data in Table 13-1 need to be converted from percentages to popular vote values. In addition, it is noticed that the Republican voters who previously voted Republican seem to fluctuate and ultimately decrease over the almost 30-year span. These two aspects are attention grabbing and are researched further in Chap. 15.

Table 13-2 presents the results from converting the percentages to absolute values. Table 13-2 entries are the calculated results of multiplying the percentages in Table 13-1 by the actual *total* voter turnout for each presidential election.

Table 13-2 Exit Poll Est. Vote and Previous Vote for Pres. Candidates by Party (M), 1972 to 2000

	1972	1980	1984	1988	1992	1996	2000
Total	77.7	86.5	92.7	91.6	104.4	96.3	105.4
Dem Dem	14.4	24.5	22.9	24.1	25.0	39.6	46.2
Dem Rep	3.6	4.0	6.1	9.0	10.8	2.9	2.0
Dem Ind	2.0	0.7	3.1	1.6	1.3	2.5	2.5
Dem Not Vote	8.2	4.2	4.4	6.1	7.8	5.3	3.7
Rep Dem	4.0	11.7	5.6	2.0	1.6	3.4	6.1
Rep Rep	33.1	25.6	43.4	42.0	32.9	24.9	29.4
Rep Ind	2.9	1.2	1.1	0.4	0.2	5.1	5.9
Rep Not Vote	8.1	5.4	5.6	5.0	5.0	2.8	3.8
Ind Dem	0.2	4.3	0.1	0.2	3.3	2.8	2.0
Ind Rep	0.3	2.7	0.2	0.6	11.3	1.5	0.8
Ind Ind	0.6	0.8	0.0	0.5	0.6	4.5	2.3
Ind Not Vote	0.4	1.5	0.0	0.2	4.7	1.2	0.7

Sources: Roper Center for Public Opinion Research National Election Day Polls (weighted samples used when available); CBS News poll, 1972, ABC News poll, 1980 to 1984; *Los Angeles Times* polls, 1988 to 2000

Before using the data from Table 13-2, the actual total Democratic candidate's votes are compared with the sum of all Democratic categories. If the exit poll sums of the Democratic categories are accurate, the two totals should track each other fairly closely. Figure 13-1 shows the actual results of the Democratic candidates along with the sum of all of the converted exit poll Democratic voter categories. Therefore, the categories Dem Dem, Dem Rep, Dem Ind, and Dem Not Vote are all summed together to obtain the exit poll totals.

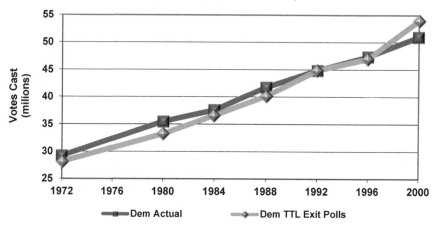

Democratic Actual and Dem TTL Votes Cast
(1972 to 2000 w/o 1976)

Sources: US Census Bureau Statistical Abstracts 2001; Roper Center for Public Opinion Research National Election Day polls (weighted samples used when available); CBS News poll, 1972, ABC News poll, 1980 to 1984; *Los Angeles Times* polls, 1988 to 2000

Figure 13-1 Democratic Actual and Dem TTL Votes Cast
(1972 to 2000 w/o 1976)

Totaling the categories with relatively close results is a partial verification of the process of converting percentages to the estimated popular vote amount. Although there are slight discrepancies, the totals for the Democratic categories seem to track the actual results. Therefore, there exists a comfortable level with the exit poll technique, and the analysis could continue.

Returning attention back to Table 13-2, instead of percentages for Dem Dem, for example, the Dem Dem row contains the estimated *number* of voters who voted for the Democratic candidate and voted for the Democratic candidate in the previous election. Once again, the Dem Dem row displays a steadily increasing amount with the exception of 1980. The larger value for the 1980 election is not a tremendous surprise since it was the first election after the 1976 anomaly. Essentially, there is an abnormal increase in the vote for the Democratic candidate in 1976 that affected the percentage of voters who voted for the previous Democratic candidate (Dem Dem). After 1980, the voting trend returned back to its consistent increase from election to election.

The Republican voters who previously voted Republican (Rep Rep), once again did not consistently show a trend. The data indicate that the voters for the Dem Dem and Rep Rep voters tend to follow the actual voters for Democratic and Republican candidates.

Nonetheless, how did the exit poll data compare with the actual results on a graph? Figure 13-2 plots the actual Democratic votes cast and the Dem Dem generated from the exit polls.

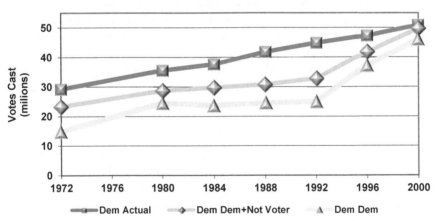

Sources: US Census Bureau Statistical Abstracts 2001; Roper Center for Public Opinion Research National Election Day polls (weighted samples used when available); CBS News poll, 1972, ABC News poll, 1980 to 1984; *Los Angeles Times* polls, 1988 to 2000.

Figure 13-2 Democratic/Dem Dem/Dem Dem+NV Votes Cast
(1972 to 2000 w/o 1976)

The graph shows three data lines: 1) the top data line depicts the actual results; 2) the bottom line includes data voters who voted for and previously voted for the Democratic candidate; and 3) the center line contains the voters of the bottom line plus the voters who voted for the Democratic candidate but did "Not Vote" in the previous presidential election. These "Not Voters" were made up of mostly first-time voters.

Even though there is a slight difference, the exit poll data from Dem Dem seems to parallel the actual election results of the Democratic candidates' voters. When "Not Voters" are added to the Dem Dem voters, the data line appears to become more linear. In fact, regression analysis reveals r^2 values of .875 for Dem Dem, .889 when Not Voters are added, and .997 for the actual election results from 1972 to 2000. As Chap. 7 explains, the closer r^2 is to the value of one, the more linear or straighter the line will be. Each of these values indicates a linear or straight-line set of data points. Although the exit polls reveal a linear trend for the Dem Dem voters, it is not as linear as the actual results. The possible difference could be the error in exit polls. It could be that true Dem Dem data follow a similar linear pattern as actual votes; however, the error in the exit poll sample may have shifted the data points to a less linear trend.

Regardless of whether the values for the Dem Dem votes do not exactly mimic the actual results, they validate the trend theory. That is to say, that the bulk of the Democratic voters were repeatedly voting for the Democratic candidate from election to election with additional new voters added. In addition, these voters continued to increase in a linear manner from election to election. Next, a review of the Republican voters that previously voted for Republican candidates.

Figure 13-3 plots the actual Republican votes cast and the Rep Rep voters with and without the previous "Not Voters." Once again, the graph shows three data lines. Again, each of the data lines closely approximates the shape of the actual Republican candidates' votes. In addition, the votes cast each category fluctuate and do not trend in a linear manner.

The third graph reviewed is for the Independent voters. Figure 13-4 plots the actual Independent votes cast and the Ind Ind voters with and without the "Not Voters" (NV). For the most part, each of the Independent data lines conform to one another. The exception is 1992.

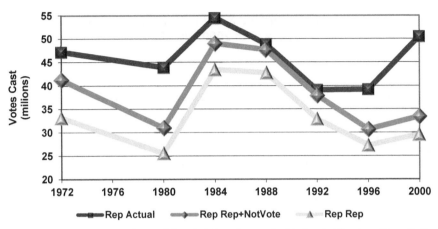

Republican, Rep Rep, Rep Rep plus NV Votes Cast (1972 to 2000 w/o 1976)

Sources: Roper Center for Public Opinion Research National Election Day Polls (weighted samples used when available); CBS News poll, 1972, ABC News Poll, 1980 to 1984; *Los Angeles Times* polls, 1988 to 2000

Figure 13-3 Republican/Rep Rep/Rep Rep+NV Votes Cast
(1972 to 2000 w/o 1976)

In 1992, the Independent candidate (Ross Perot) did not pull most of his votes from new voters or voters who previously voted for the Independent candidate. The majority of his voters came from those that previously voted for Democratic or Republican candidate. The largest amount, over 11 million, came from those who previously voted for the Republican candidate (George H. W. Bush). The remaining, about 3.3 million, came from those that previously voted for the Democratic candidate (Michael Dukakis) and 4.7 million did not previously vote.

Next, voters who swung between the Republican candidates and the Independent candidates are reviewed. Prior to reviewing this graph, the hypothesis is that if the voters who voted repeatedly for the Republican candidates and occasionally for the Democratic candidate were removed from the total Republican voters, what should be left would be those that swung back and forth between Republican and Independent candidates (see Fig. 13-5). Republican voters who were left included Republican voters who previously voted for the Independent candidate plus Republican voters who previously did not vote. Independent voters who were left included Independent voters who previously voted for the Republican candidate plus Independent voters who previously did not vote.

Independent, Ind Ind & Ind Ind plus NV Votes Cast (1972 to 2000 w/o 1976)

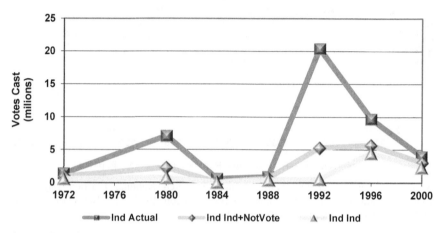

Sources: Roper Center for Public Opinion Research National Election Day Polls (weighted samples used when available); CBS News poll, 1972, ABC News poll, 1980 to 1984; *Los Angeles Times* polls, 1988 to 2000

Figure 13-4 Independent, Ind Ind & Ind Ind+NV Votes Cast
(1972 to 2000 w/o 1976)

These two different types of voters should show a *mirroring* pattern since they were vying for the same voters in existed in the theoretical non-Democratic electorate. It is expected that the mirroring would not be as identical as the actual Republican and Independent results show. Figure 13-5 displays the Republican voters who switched back and forth between Republican and Independent candidates. As suspected, there exists a mirroring of the two types of voters. Also, as expected, the two types of voters did not reflect as much of an identical mirroring as the actual data (see Fig. 4-6). Why did this occur?

The central reason is that the actual mirror effect incorporates all voters who voted for the Republican candidates and all voters who voted for Independent candidates. In order to get a true mirroring, all voter categories must be included because the candidate is pulling voters away from all of the categories. In each election, the Republican candidate pulled voters away who consisted of more than the voters who voted previously from for the Independent candidate. Moreover, the Independent candidate pulled voters away who consisted of more than voters who previously voted for the Republican candidate.

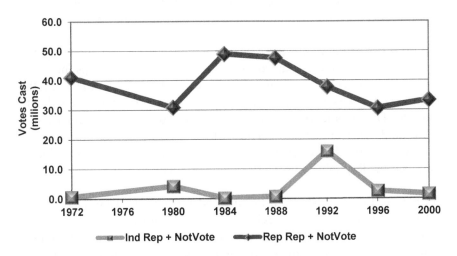

Sources: Roper Center for Public Opinion Research National Election Day Polls (weighted samples used when available); CBS News poll, 1972, ABC News poll, 1980 to 1984; *Los Angeles Times* polls, 1988 to 2000

Figure 13-5 Rep Rep + NV/Ind Rep +NV Votes Cast
(1972 to 2000 w/o 1976)

In 1992, it is clear that the Republican voters who previously voted for the Republican candidate deceased slightly less than the Independent voter who previously voted for the Republican candidate vice versa (8 million decrease for Rep Rep while 9.7 million increase of Ind Rep). The more interesting election is 1996. The 1996 election shows a decrease for both the Rep Rep and the Ind Rep categories. This clearly shows that a significant amount of Republican voters did not vote for the Republican or Independent candidates in the 1996 election. Reviewing the exit poll data also reveals that a substantial amount of them did not vote for the Democratic candidate as well.

The Swing Voters Who Vote Democratic

From the beginning of the development of the presidential trend theory, there had always been an assumption that there existed a group of voters who swung back and forth between the two fractured electorates. The exit polls reveal that the Democratic voters who previously voted for the Democratic candidate (Dem Dem) increased in a linear fashion (see Fig. 13-2). However, what occurred to the remaining portion that swung back and forth between the Democratic and non-Democratic electorates?

Figure 13-6 contains the three major voting groups that made up the Democratic electorate extracted from the exit polls. The groups include 1) the total Democratic vote of all Dem categories (Dem TTL); 2) the Democratic voters who previously voted for the Democratic candidate plus the Democratic voters who previously did not vote (Dem Dem + NV); and 3) Democratic voters who previously voted for a non-Democratic candidate (Dem ND); the non-Democratic candidates included the Republican or Independent candidates.

As before, Fig. 13-6 shows a linear trend for both the Dem Dem voters (Democratic voters who previously voted Democratic) and the total Democratic vote. In addition, the Democratic voters who previously voted for a non-Democratic candidate (Republican or Independent) seem to mirror the Dem Dem voters. In addition, the number of these voters seems to be relatively consistent. In fact, its trend line, which is in the dashed line, is relatively horizontal from 1972 to 2000.

A *consistent* group of voters who swung between the non-Democratic and Democratic candidates is part of the conditions required for the Democratic votes cast to be linear. The consistency and the configuration of the votes cast from the Democratic voters who previously voted for a non-Democratic candidate provides the essence of why the total Democratic vote is linear.

The consistent group of voters made up the difference between the number of Dem Dem+NV voters and actual votes cast. Essentially, since these voters are consistent, they simply increased the number of voters to the level of actual voters and kept the trend linear (see Fig. 13-6). Further proof is shown viewing the red dashed trend line in the graph that is flat and constant throughout 1972 to 2000.

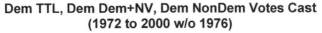

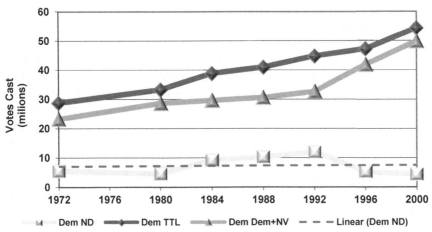

Sources: Roper Center for Public Opinion Research National Election Day Polls (weighted samples used when available); CBS News poll, 1972, ABC News poll, 1980 to 1984; *Los Angeles Times* polls, 1988 to 2000

Figure 13-6 Dem TTL/Dem Dem+NV/Dem NonDem Votes Cast
(1972 to 2000 w/o 1976)

Consequently, other than the original graph of 1-5, Figure 13-6 could possibly be the *most* important graph for the presidential trend. The results of the linear Dem Dem+NV and consistent Dem ND voters **corroborate** a critical aspect of the presidential trend theory. That is to say, that votes for the Democratic candidate after 1972 were comprised of Democratic voters who repeatedly voted for the Democratic candidate plus a collection of new voters plus a consistent group of voters who voted for both Democratic and non-Democratic candidates (see Chap. 1). Consequently, the data from exit polls validate the isolation or existence of the Democratic electorate.

Originally, it was thought that when the fracturing of the presidential electorate occurred in 1972 it left *only* Democratic base or core voters in the Democratic electorate. Hence, the cause of the linearity of the vote increases from election to election. However, using the analysis from the exit polls, the popular vote for the Democratic candidate is actually made up of base or core voters who repeatedly voted for the Democratic candidate plus a *consistent* amount of voters who swung back and forth from the Democratic candidates and non-Democratic candidate.

Proving the Baseline Theory with Exit Polls

Exit poll data have revealed that the Democratic voters who previously voted for the Democratic candidates increased in a linear fashion similar to the actual vote (see Fig. 13-1). This was initially postulated when the theory was developing (see Chap. 1). Thus, the exit polls validated that the vote for the Democratic candidate consisted largely of Democratic voters who continued to vote for the Democratic candidate from election to election plus a batch of new voters. Exit polls also showed that remaining Democratic voters consisted of a relatively *consistent* number of voters that swung between the theoretical Democratic electorate and non-Democratic electorate.

Exit polls have also validated the mirroring of the Republican voters who previously voted for the Independent candidate, and the Independent voters who previously voted for the Republican candidate tended to mirror each other (see Fig. 13-4). Thus, exit polls again corroborated that these two were isolated in separate electorates.

However, can exit poll data validate the baseline? For a refresher, the baselines are revealed using the 1948, 1968, and 1992 elections. Although it is believed that there was a shifting or dropping off of the Democratic baseline in 1972 (see Chap. 9), the three election years approximated the baseline.

Nevertheless, there are several problems with viewing the baselines using exit poll data. First, relevant exit poll data are not available for 1948 and 1968. Also, there is only one exit poll category that should contain the baseline voters. The baseline voters should be contained in the exit poll category that indicates the previous voter voting for the same party. These are the voters who repeatedly voted for the candidate of the same party, election after election. Thus, the Dem Dem should have contained the baseline voters for the Democratic voters, and the Rep Rep should have contained the baseline voters for the Republican candidates. The same three elections for the Independent voters (Ind Ind) would not be relevant; since there is no indication of a significant baseline or continuous previous Independent voters, it reveals a maximum and not a baseline.

Now here lies the problem with the Democratic candidate's baseline. The Dem Dem for the 1968 election is not available. However, there was an election where by the popular vote was extremely close to the popular vote for 1968. That election was 1972. Therefore, the hypothesis is that the votes for the Dem Dem voters for 1972 should be close to the Democratic candidates' baseline. Thus, the number of Dem Dem voters for 1972 could be used to estimate the number for 1968.

Since the Dem Dem amount relies on the number of previous voters, it is important to use elections where the prior election's Democratic votes were *not* substantially higher than the election used. If the votes were substantially higher for the previous election, it would most likely include a significant amount of another party's votes. The election of 1972 fits the bill. The Democratic candidate vote casts in 1968 was not substantially different from the 1972 election. Also, the 1988 election was not substantially different from the 1992 election.

There is one final problem: what value should be used for the 1948 election? This is where another important determination is made. Since it is theorized that the initial fracturing of the electorate began in 1948 (see Chap. 2), maybe the starting point should be zero? Hence, from the 1948 election on, the Dem Dem baseline for the Democratic candidates would grow in a linear manner according to the addition of new voting population (with the possible exception of the shift in 1968 to 1972).

Validation of this new hypothesis would be the presence of a near linear line for the Dem Dem vote for elections of 1948, 1972, and 1992. To reiterate, the election of 1972 is used because of the vote similarity and the unavailability of 1968 data. Figure 13-7 shows such a near linear trend line for 1948, 1972, and 1992.

In fact, the r^2 value for the Dem Dem baseline is .9742 versus .9837 for the total Democratic baseline of 1948, 1968, and 1992. Both are very linear values. Since 1972 is used, it is unclear whether the trend would have a greater linearity if 1968 is substituted in place of 1972. That being said, the Dem Dem baseline with 1972 is linear and seems to possess the slight bend upward similar to the original total Democratic baseline.

However, there is no way to determine the Dem Dem value for 1968 to reflect the same shift as the total votes cast.

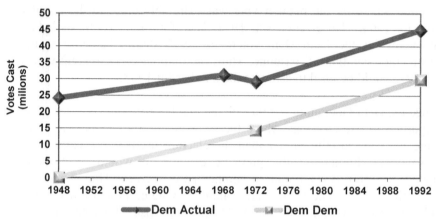

Dem Actual & Dem Dem Pres. Votes Cast (1948, 1968, 1972, 1992)

Sources: US Census Bureau Statistical Abstracts 1951 to 2004 and uselectionatlas.org

Figure 13-7 Dem Actual & Dem Dem Baseline w/Shift (1948, 1968, 1972, 1992)

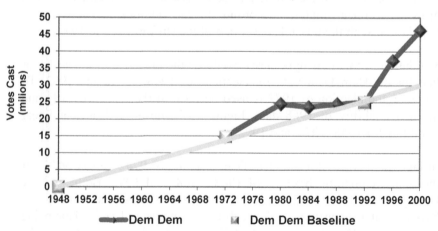

Dem Dem Presidential Vote Cast & Extended Baseline (1948, 1972 to 2000)

Sources: US Census Bureau Statistical Abstracts 1951 to 2004 and uselectionatlas.org

Figure 13-8 Dem Dem Pres. Vote/Baseline (1948, 1972 to 2000)

When the additional elections from 1980 to 2000 are plotted on the graph, the results agree with the baseline theory (see Fig. 13-8). That is, if Dem Dem vote of 1948, 1972 (replaced from 1968), and 1992 define the baseline trend, they should be the lowest points on the graphs. A review of Fig. 13-8 shows that there were no elections with Dem Dem votes cast lower than the Dem Dem baseline trend. This trend line represents the true baseline or lowest vote total that the Democratic candidate should obtain. It also brings credibility to the theory that the initial *crack* of the presidential voting electorate occurred in 1948 (see Chap. 2).

In contrast to the Democratic baseline, the Republican Rep Rep baseline is configured such that it is difficult to determine. The Republican candidates' votes cast included mostly Republican and Independent voters while the Democratic candidates included mostly only Democratic voters. Thus, since the Rep Rep votes cast included Independent voters, it is difficult to locate baseline elections where the previous election contained only or mostly Republican voters for the Republican candidate. Therefore, the Rep Rep baseline cannot be defined.

Finally, it is most likely the starting point for a new type of voter. *The election of 1948 is probably the starting point for Democratic and most likely Republican core voters in presidential elections.* The election of 1948 may have just barely cracked the electorate; however, it may possibly have created the group of voters known as core voters at the presidential level.

Trend Demographics for the Democratic Candidates

Since the trend for the total popular vote has been shown to exist, one may assume that it may have manifested for demographic subgroups as well. The hypothesis is that each demographic group should show some type of linear trend for the Democratic candidate's vote.

Exit poll data percentages are obtained for the major race/ethnicity groups (white, black, Hispanic, and Asian). Table 13-3 includes the data collected for the analysis. [101] These percentages reflect the portion of the race/ethnicity group that voted for the Democratic candidates.

---

[101] Exit poll data did not indicate whether data was non-Hispanic white, black, or Asian or whether it included Hispanic population in the race counts.

Table 13-3 Exit Polls Votes Cast for Dem. Candidates by Race/Ethnicity, %
1972 to 2000, w/o 1976

	1972	1980	1984	1988	1992	1996	2000
White Dem, % (poll)	31	36	34	40	39	43	42
Black Dem, % (poll)	82	85	90	86	83	84	90
Hisp., Dem, % (poll)	63	56	62	69	61	72	62
Asian Dem, % (poll)					31	43	54

Sources: New York Times exit poll data (1972 to 2000) and Edison Media Research Mitofsky International

Using the exit poll percentages in Table 13-3 as well as the actual voter turnout data, the estimated votes cast by major race/ethnicity group (white, black, Hispanic, and Asian) are calculated (see Table 13-4).

Table 13-4 Est. Votes Cast for Democratic Candidates by Race/Ethnicity,
1972 to 2000, w/o 1976
(%/millions)

	1972	1980	1984	1988	1992	1996	2000
TO Turnout (M)	77.7	86.5	92.7	91.6	104.4	96.3	105.4
White TO, % (poll)	90	89	87	85	87	83	81
Black TO, % (poll)	8	10	9	10	8	10	10
Hisp. TO, % (poll)	2	2	2	3	2	5	6
Asian TO, % (poll)					1	1	2
White Dem est. (M)	21.6	27.7	27.4	31.1	35.4	34.4	35.9
Black Dem est. (M)	5.1	7.4	7.5	7.9	6.9	8.1	9.5
Hisp. Dem est. (M)	1.2	1.0	1.1	1.9	1.3	3.5	3.9
Asian Dem est. (M)					0.3	0.4	1.1

Source: *New York Times* Exit Poll data (1980 to 2000); Voter Registration and Turnout in Federal Elections by Race/Ethnicity 1972 to 1996 (for 1972 turnout, %); Votes cast calculations
Note: TO = Turnout; M = Millions

The Democratic vote for each race/Ethnicity group is calculated using the following formula:

$$RaceDem = TO * RaceTO\% * RaceDem\%$$

Where:

RaceDem = Race/Ethnicity Democratic Turnout;
TO = Total Turnout;
RaceTO% = % Turnout of Race/Ethnicity group of the total turnout;
RaceDem% = % of Race/Ethnicity group turnout voting Democratic

The initial graph to investigate contained the minority population (Race/ethnicity). The estimated votes cast for each major minority group are plotted and can be seen in Fig. 13-9 showing the vote for the Democratic candidates by each of the major race/ethnicity group. The first thing to note is that all major minority groups show an increasing trend fairly similar to the one reflected for the total Democratic vote. However, there is a noticeable dip in the 1992 election by African Americans and Hispanic/Latinos.

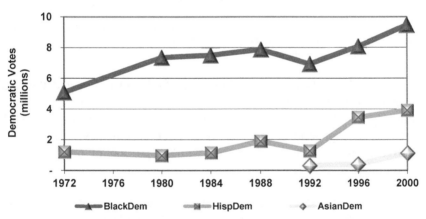

Minority Democratic Votes Cast (1972 to 2000 w/o 1976)

Sources: New York Times Exit Poll Data (1972-2000), US Census Bureau Current Population Survey, 2000 & Voting & Registration in the November Election

Figure 13-9 Minority Democratic Votes Cast (1972 to 2000 w/o 1976)

Regardless of the dip, since the total votes cast for the Democratic candidates votes cast are linear, then the sum of all of the population groups must also be linear. How could that be the case when both African American and Hispanic/Latino population dips visibly in 1992?

Could the white population correct this dip? To answer this question, the major minority groups are displayed along with voters who are white.

Table 13-5 presents the estimated votes cast for the Democratic candidate by white and minority population groups. Using these data, Fig. 13-10 is created. What Fig. 13-10 and Table 13-5 reveal is that the dip of the minority voters in 1992 is offset by an increase in white voters.

Table 13-5 Est. White & Minority Votes Cast for the Democratic Candidate, 1972 to 2000 (millions)

	1972	1980	1984	1988	1992	1996	2000
TtlTurnout Actual (M)	77.7	86.5	92.7	91.6	104.4	96.3	105.4
WhiteTO est. (M)	69.9	77.0	80.6	77.9	90.8	79.9	85.4
MinTO est. (M)	7.8	9.5	12.0	13.7	13.6	16.4	20.0
DemTO Actual (M)	29.2	35.5	37.6	41.8	44.9	47.4	51.0
WhiteDemTO est. (M)	21.6	27.7	27.4	31.1	35.4	34.4	35.9
MinDemTO est. (M)	7.6	7.8	10.2	10.7	9.5	13.0	15.1

Sources: New York Times Exit Poll data (1980 to 2000); Voter Registration and Turnout in Federal Elections by Race/Ethnicity 1972 to 1996 (for 1972 turnout, %)
Note: TO = Turnout; M = Millions

In fact, both the Democratic white votes (WhiteDemTO) and the total turnout of white votes (WhiteTO) increased while the Democratic minority votes (MinDemTO) and total minority votes (MinTO) decreased. Apparently, the three major candidates significantly motivated white voters to turn out while a portion of minority votes stayed home.

It is apparent that the increase and decrease for the white and minority voters in 1992 tend to cancel each other out for the Democratic candidate, Bill Clinton. Bill Clinton received an increase of 4.3 million white voters from the previous Democratic candidate (Michael Dukakis), while he received 1.2 million less minority voters. Summing the two equates to a 3.1 million increase in total voters overall for the Democratic candidate. The 3.1 million voter amount is the same amount as the average trend line increase from 1984 to 2000. Therefore, although there is a dip in minority votes cast, total trend continued to progress in a linear manner. Nonetheless, it is notable that both the white and minority population increased in a relatively consistent trend (see Demographic trend lines, below).

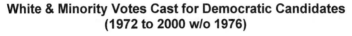

White & Minority Votes Cast for Democratic Candidates (1972 to 2000 w/o 1976)

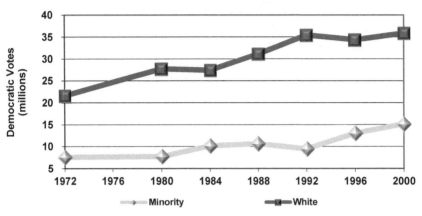

Sources: *New York Times* Exit Poll Data (1972 to 2000), US Census Bureau Current Population Survey, 2000 & Voting & Registration in the November Election

Figure 13-10 White & Minority Democratic Votes Cast (1972 to 2000, w/o 1976)

Figure 13-10 led to a question of how the non-Democratic side would fair. Consequently, tables and graphs are developed to reflect the non-Democratic candidate's votes.

Trend Demographics of the Non-Democratic Candidates

As with the Democratic candidates, the votes cast by race/ethnicity is determined using exit poll data. This time, since exit poll data did not include non-Democrats, the Democratic values were used as a basis to calculate the non-Democratic values. In essence, the non-Democratic candidates votes included all voters who were *not* Democratic voters. For instance, if the black voters voted 90 percent for the Democratic candidate, then the non-Democratic candidates received 10 percent of the black vote.

Table 13-6 is developed to include the race/ethnicity breakdown by race/ethnicity for 1972 to 2000. In this instance, the table shows the percentages that reflect the portion of the race/ethnicity group who voted for the non-Democratic candidates.

Table 13-6 Est. Votes Cast for Non-Democratic Candidates by Race/Ethnicity 1972 to 2000

	1972	1980	1984	1988	1992	1996	2000
WhiteNDem, % est.	69	64	66	60	61	57	58
BlackNDem, % est.	18	15	10	14	17	16	10
HispNDem, % est.	37	44	38	31	39	28	38
AsianNDem, % est.					69	57	46

Sources: New York Times exit poll data (1972 to 2000)/Edison Media Research Mitofsky International
Note: TO = Turnout; M = Millions

Using exit poll percentages in Table 13-6 as well as the actual voter turnout data, the estimated votes cast by major race/ethnicity group (white, black, Hispanic, and Asian) are calculated (see Table 13-7).

The non-Democratic vote for each major race/ethnicity group is calculated using the following formula:

$$RaceNDem = TO * RaceTO\% * RaceNDem\%$$

Where:

$RaceNDem$ = Race/Ethnicity Non-Democratic Turnout;
TO = Total Turnout;
$RaceTO\%$ = % Turnout of Race/Ethnicity of the total turnout;
$RaceNDem\%$ = % of Race/Ethnicity turnout voting non-Democratic

Using data from Table 13-7, Fig. 13-11 is created, which graphs the trend of each major minority race/ethnicity. In addition, as before, the minority groups are collapsed into one category. The results are provided in Table 13-8.

Table 13-7 Est. Votes Cast for Non-Democratic Candidates by Race/Ethnicity, 1972 to 2000
(%/millions)

	1972	1980	1984	1988	1992	1996	2000
Turnout (Actual)	77.7	86.5	92.7	91.6	104.4	96.3	105.4
WhiteTO, % (poll)	90	89	87	85	87	83	81
BlackTO, % (poll)	8%	10	9	10	8	10	10
HispanicTO, % (poll)	2	2	2	3	2	5	6
AsianTO, % (poll)					1	1	2
WhiteNDem, est. (M)	48.0	49.3	53.2	46.7	55.4	45.5	49.5
BlackNDem, est. (M)	1.1	1.3	0.8	1.3	1.4	1.5	1.1
HispNDem, est. (M)	0.7	0.8	0.7	0.9	0.8	1.3	2.4
AsianNDem, est. (M)					0.7	0.5	1.0

Sources: *New York Times* exit poll data (1980 to 2000); Census Voting and Registration in Federal Elections 1972 (for 1972 turnout, %); votes cast calculations
Note: TO = Turnout; M = Millions

Minority Non-Democratic Votes Cast
(1972 to 2000 w/o 1976)

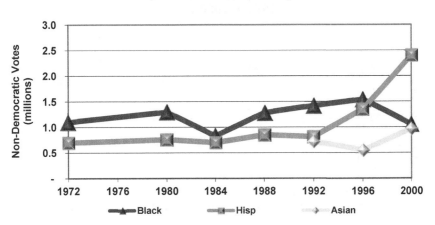

Sources: *New York Times* exit poll data (1972 to 2000), US Census Bureau Current Population Survey, 2000 & Voting & Registration in the November Election

Figure 13-11 Minority Non-Democratic Votes Cast
(1972 to 2000, w/o 1976)

Table 13-8 Est. White & Minority Votes Cast for the Non-Dem Candidate, 1972 to 2000 (millions)

	1972	1980	1984	1988	1992	1996	2000
Ttl. Turnout Actual (M)	77.7	86.5	92.7	91.6	104.4	96.3	105.4
WhtTO, est. (M)	69.9	77.0	80.6	77.9	90.8	79.9	85.4
MinTO, est. (M)	7.8	9.5	12.0	13.7	13.6	16.4	20.0
NDemTO Actual (M)	48.6	51.0	55.1	49.8	59.5	48.9	54.4
WhtNDemTO, est. (M)	48.0	49.3	53.2	46.7	55.4	45.5	49.5
MinNDemTO, est. (M)	0.5	1.8	1.9	3.1	4.1	3.3	4.9

Source: New York Times exit poll data (1972 to 2000); votes cast calculations
Note: TO = Turnout; M = Millions; Dem = Democratic voters

The next item created is Fig. 13-12, which consists of two lines: the white and minority non-Democratic turnout. One of the first items noted from Fig. 13-12 is that votes cast of white voters for the non-Democratic candidates has been stable from 1972 to 2000.

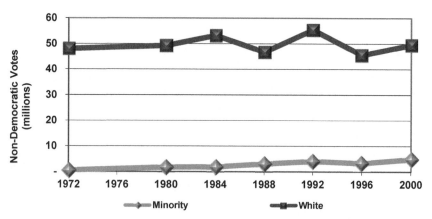

White & Minority Non-Democratic Votes Cast (1972 to 2000 w/o 1976)

Sources: New York Times exit poll data (1972 to 2000); US Census Bureau Current Population Survey, 2000 & Voting & Registration in the November Election

Figure 13-12 White/Minority Non-Democratic Votes Cast (1972 – 2000, w/o 1976)

In 1972, the white non-Democratic votes cast was 48 million while in 2000 it had grown to only 49.5 million. The minority votes cast were a half million in 1972 and 4.9 million in 2000. The total non-Democratic growth was similar. In 1972, the non-Democratic turnout was 48.6 million in 1972 and 54.4 million in 2000. A visible indication of the stability of the white and minority voters can be seen in Fig. 13-12.

This slight increase is substantially different from the increase in the Democratic candidates white/minority race categories. Figure 13-13 shows the comparison between the Democratic and non-Democratic candidates' votes cast. Clearly, votes cast for the Democratic White/minority race categories increased much greater than those of the non-Democratic.

White & Minority Dem/Non-Dem Votes Cast
(1972 to 2000 w/o 1976)

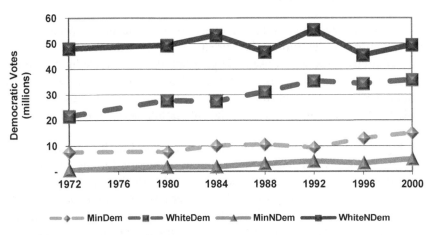

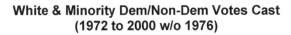

Sources: *New York Times* exit poll data (1980 to 2000); US Census Bureau Current Population Survey, 2000 & Voting & Registration in the November Election

Figure 13-13 White & Minority Dem/Non-Dem Votes Cast
(1972 to 2000, w/o 1976)

Figure 13-13 shows the significant increase from 1972 to 2000 of white voters for the Democratic candidates of 14.3 million and a minor increase of the non-Democratic candidates of 1.5 million. It also shows the increase of 7.5 million minority voters for the Democratic candidates and increase of 4.5 million non-Democratic candidates. Collectively, these graphs show something stark for the two theoretical electorates.

The graphs reveal that the Democratic electorate expanded considerably from 1972 to 2000 while the non-Democratic electorate has barely increased. This expansion and lack thereof are discussed in the next section, "Demographic Trend Lines."

These last few graphs may have seem to be unrelated to the presidential trend theory. However, each of the various racial groups would not be trending in a linear pattern if it were not for the fracturing of the electorate. When the fracturing occurred in 1972, it left a staunch group of core voters in the Democratic electorate. These core voters consisted of the major race/ethnicity population groups. Furthermore, these separate groups are the actual reason why the presidential trend exists. When the groups are summed together, they in turn produce a linear trend.

Demographic Trend Lines

The previous section stimulates a question. The question is promoted by the attempt to determine the direction of growth for the different race/ethnicity groups. Consequently, what do the race/ethnicity trend lines reveal about the votes cast for the Democratic and non-Democratic candidates? In order to perform this type of review, trend lines need to be added to the previous graphs, and the data points need to be dropped.

As Fig. 13-14 shows, the graph depicts the trend line for the percentage of vote cast of each major race/ethnicity category for the Democratic candidates from 1972 to 2000. Included on the graph is a clearly defined pattern for each of the groups. The pattern is that *each* race/ethnicity group increases from 1972 to 2000. This means that every major race/ethnicity group continually increased for the Democratic candidate from 1972 to 2000. Alternatively, Fig. 13-15 shows the non-Democratic candidates trend lines for race/ethnicity from 1972 to 2000. It revealed the opposite. All trend lines decrease from 1972 to 2000.

This should be extremely troubling for the Republican or Independent candidates. To repeat: Democratic candidates from 1972 to 2000 were consistently obtaining a larger percentage of the vote from every major race/ethnicity group.

Race/Ethnicity Trend Lines for Dem. Candidates, %
(1972 to 2000, w/o 1976)

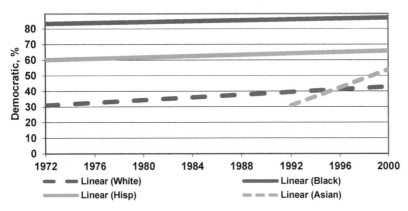

Sources: US Census Bureau Current Population Survey, 2000 & Voting & Registration in the November Election, uselectionatlas.org

Figure 13-14 Race/Ethnicity Trend Lines for Democratic Candidate, % (1972 to 2000, w/o 1976)

Race/Ethnicity Trend Lines for Non-Dem Candidates, %
(1972 to 2000, w/o 1976)

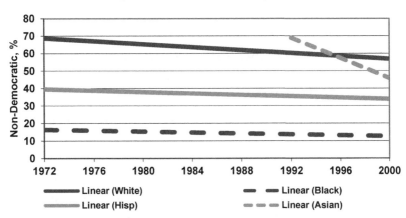

Sources: US Census Bureau Current Population Survey, 2000 & Voting & Registration in the November Election, uselectionatlas.org

Figure 13-15 Race/Ethnicity Trend Lines for Non-Democratic Candidates, % (1972 to 2000, w/o 1976)

The surprising aspect of the graphs is that the increase involved not just the minority voters for the Democratic candidates. Most political analysts would agree that minority voters were voting in greater numbers for the Democratic candidates. However, the fact that white voters were increasingly voting for the Democratic candidates and less for the non-Democratic candidates is *surprising*.

When all of the race/ethnicity groups are collapsed together, a more stark representation is provided for the Democratic and non-Democratic candidates (see Fig. 13-16).

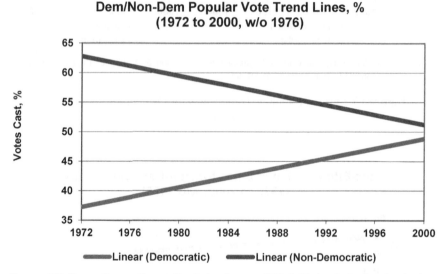

Dem/Non-Dem Popular Vote Trend Lines, %
(1972 to 2000, w/o 1976)

Sources: US Census Bureau Current Population Survey, 2000 & Voting & Registration in the November Election, uselectionatlas.org

Figure 13-16 Dem/Non-Dem Popular Vote Trend Lines, %
(1972 to 2000, w/o 1976)

Under the presidential trend theory, votes for the Democratic and non-Democratic candidates exist in two different theoretical electorates. Therefore, their votes cast can be viewed as the number of voters who turned out in the two theoretical electorates. In fact, a graph could be developed to show the increase in voters that turn out in the Democratic and non-Democratic electorates. Figure 13-17 shows a graphical image of each electorate voters compared to the total votes cast.

**Democratic & Non-Democratic % of Total Popular Vote
(1972 to 2000, w/o 1976)**

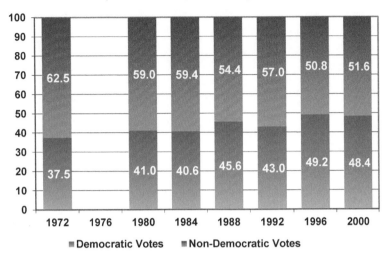

Sources: US Census Bureau Current Population Survey, 2000 & Voting & Registration in the November Election, uselectionatlas.org

Figure 13-17 Democratic & Non-Democrat Percentage of Popular Vote
(1972 to 2000, w/o 1976)

The percentage of voters who turn out is clearly trending in an increasing manner for the Democratic electorate and thus decreasing for the non-Democratic electorate. These undeniable trends bode poorly for the non-Democratic presidential candidates. However, the Democratic candidates should fair well if the electorate remained fractured and these trends continue. If you are curious about the continuation of these trends review Part 4, Chaps. 14 and 15 for additional information and the answer to that question and more.

Analysis of the Trend Using Exit Polls

PART 5

Post-Trend Analysis

Chapter 14

The End of the Trend?

Introduction

A question that may be lingering while reading of this book is what occurred after 2000? Excluding the 1976 election, we know that the Democratic candidates' popular vote increased in a consistent pattern for almost three decades. As previously stated, this is an amazing phenomenon when considering the different candidates, different current issues, varying voter turnout percentages, and more. Nonetheless, through all of these differing conditions and circumstances, the Democratic popular vote for president continued to increase in a predictable fashion.

However, did the trend end in 2000? Of course the answer to this question resides with the elections of 2004, 2008, and 2012. This chapter discusses the end of the trend as a potential expansion of the Democratic electorate.

The 2004, 2008, and 2012 Elections

One of the easiest ways to view whether the trend continues is to add the 2004, 2008, and 2012 popular vote to the graph of the trend (see Fig. 14-1). When viewing the trend from 1972 to 2012, undeniably the popular vote for the Democratic candidate begins to deviate from the trend line in 2004.

Furthermore, extending the trend line from 1972 to 2000, the projected popular vote for 2004 should have been close to 54 million (see Table 14-1). However, the actual popular vote ended up being 59 million. The 2004 projection underestimates the popular vote by over 5 million votes. Likewise, the popular vote for the Democratic candidate for president in

2008 was 12 million votes more than the estimated amount using the 1972 to 2000 trend line.

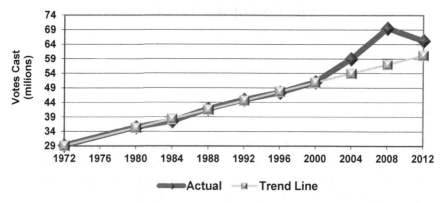

Actual vs. Trend Line of the Democratic Popular Vote (1972 to 2012 w/o 1976)

Sources: US Census Bureau Statistical Abstracts 2010 and uselectionatlas.org

Figure 14-1 Actual Versus Trend Line of the Democratic Popular Vote
(1972 to 2012, w/o 1976)

Although the estimated amount for 2004 remains reasonably precise and continues to validate the trend, the deviation is notable. In fact, the accuracy of the 1972 to 2000 trend line projection for the 2004 election is fairly low yet somewhat respectable at 90.6 percent (see Table 14-1). On the other hand, the 2008 estimated amount is a poor 78.2 percent accurate. When the 2012 election is reviewed, the trend line estimate seems to be more in line with the actual votes cast.

Once the accuracies of the trend lines are compared, the elections of 2004, 2008, and 2012 once again noticeably stand out (see Fig. 14-2). The trend line estimates for 1972 to 2000 are all accurate while the 2004 through 2012 all seem to drop off. Although a case could possibly be made that the 2004 election was a slight anomaly, and the presidential trend continued. The election of 2008 is undeniable. The trend clearly has ended.

Table 14-1 Popular Vote for the Democratic Candidate
and the Estimated Amount, 2004 to 2012
(millions)

	2004
Actual Popular Vote	59.0
Trend line Estimation (1972 to 2000)	54.0
Accuracy, %	90.6
	2008
Actual Popular Vote	69.5
Trend line Estimation (1972 to 2000)	57.1
Accuracy, %	78.2
	2012
Actual Popular Vote	65.2
Trend line Estimation (1972 to 2000	60.2
Accuracy, %	91.6

Sources: US Census Bureau Statistical Abstracts 2010; uselectionatlas.org; Trend calculations

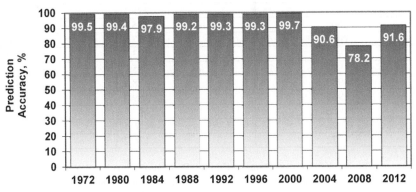

Accuracy% of 1972 - 2000 Trend Line Estimates
Democractic Candidate
(1972 to 2012 w/o 1976)

Source: Presidential Trend Analysis

Figure 14-2 Accuracy of Trend Line Estimates, Democratic Candidates, %
(1972 to 2012 w/o 1976)

Why are the predicted values and accuracies so much lower than the others? Or, better stated, why is the actual popular vote much higher? The next section attempts to answer this question.

Why a Step-Level Increase in Popular Vote After 2000?

In determining why there was an increase in popular vote, the question arose whether there was an increase in the turnout of voters or was there an increase in the overall voting age population of the country? To answer this question, the US Census Bureau's Current Population Survey's Supplement on Voting and Registration is reviewed. This survey is useful from the point that it provides an estimate of voting age population, registration, and voter turnout for presidential election years. Although voter turnout from the survey is an estimate, the critical piece of this analysis centers on comparison and not on any specific or actual amount.

Nonetheless, according to the survey, there is an increase in the voting age population of over 13 million persons from the November 2000 general election to the November 2004 election (see Table 14-2).

Table 14-2 US Voting Age Population (VAP) Increase, 1972 to 2012 (millions)

Year	VAP	Increase
2012*	233.9	8.4
2008	225.5	9.8
2004	**215.7**	**13.1**
2000	202.6	9.0
1996	193.7	8.0
1992	185.7	7.6
1988	178.1	8.1
1984	169.9	12.9
1980	157.1	10.5
1976	146.5	10.3
1972	136.2	19.7

Sources: Source: US Census Bureau, Current Population Surveys 1968 to 2008; US Census Bureau Population Estimates. *2012 extrapolated using 2008 and 2010 CPS Data

Note: Values are rounded to the nearest single decimal point.

Excluding 1972, 2004 shows the largest increase in over 30 years. The year 1972 increases most likely due to the 26th Amendment, which was passed in July 1971. The 26th Amendment bars the states or federal government from setting a voting age higher than 18. This led to an unusual increase in voting age population. Prior to, some states increased their voting age to 21 years. When the 26th Amendment was enacted, these individuals in those states who were between 18 and 21 were now able to vote and now considered part of the voting age population.

However, the dramatic increase of 2004, which significantly differed from recent years, led to the belief that the increase in the Democratic candidate's vote is linked to the unusual increase in voting age population from 2000 to 2004. At the same time, it is noticed that the elections of 1972 to 1984 display fairly high increases. In order for there to be an extraordinary increase in 2004 the elections years with similar increase must not have translated into an increase in turnout. Therefore, did these other election cycles have a substantial increase in turnout?

Before reviewing the increases in voter turnout, the voting age population should have translated into an increase in voter registration (see Table 14-3).

Table 14-3 Voter Registration Increase, 1972 to 2012 (millions)

Year	Registered	Increase
2012	na	na
2008	146.3	4.2
2004	**142.1**	**12.6**
2000	129.5	1.8
1996	127.7	1.1
1992	126.6	8.0
1988	118.6	2.5
1984	116.1	11.1
1980	105.0	7.3
1976	97.7	-.7[102]
1972	98.5	11.9

Sources: US Census Bureau, Current Population Surveys 1968 to 2008; Voting & Registration Tables

---

[102] There was a decrease in the number of registered voters from 1972 to 1976.

Therefore, registration data are obtained, and the increases from presidential elections to presidential elections are calculated and reviewed similar to the voting age population.

Reviewing the increase in registered voters again shows a similar finding as the voting age population. The increase in registered voters from 2000 to 2004 was the largest increase in 30 years.

To be specific, over 12 million new registered voters were added from 2000 to 2004. The previous two presidential election cycles (1992 to 1996 and 1996 to 2000) added only 1.1 million and 1.8 million, respectively. Clearly, the 2000 to 2004 cycle is substantially larger than the increase of any in recent years. This time only 1972 and 1984 had similar increases instead of 1972 through 1984. However, did the 1972 and 1984 increases translate into an increase in turnout?

The next step is to review the increase in turnout of the voters since 1972. [103] A review of voter turnout data for presidential elections yielded similar result as the voting age population and registration (see Table 14-4).

Table 14-4 Presidential Voter Turnout Increase, 1972 to 2012 (millions)

Year	Voter Turnout	Increase
2012	125.5	-5.8
2008	131.1	5.4
2004	**125.7**	**14.9**
2000	110.8	5.8
1996	105.0	-8.8
1992	113.9	11.6
1988	102.2	0.3
1984	101.9	8.8
1980	93.1	6.4
1976	86.7	0.9
1972	85.8	6.8

Sources: US Census Bureau Current Population Survey, 1968-2008 & Voting & Registration Tables; uselectionatlas.org

---

[103] Since the current population survey samples the voting population, the actual turnout for the elections differ from the estimated amounts.

Once again, the election cycle from 2000 to 2004 had the highest increase in turnout since 1972. The turnout of voters increased almost 15 million from 2000 to 2004. Only 1992 came close to the increase from presidential election to presidential election with over 11 million, up from 1988. In addition, none of the election from 1972 to 1984 shows the same substantial turnout increase that was prevalent with the voting age population or registration.

The increase or lack thereof is apparent when all three increase-columns are included on the same table. In Table 14-5, the increase in voting age population, registration, and turnout are all placed together side by side.

Table 14-5 Presidential VAP, Reg. Voter & Turnout Inc., 1972 to 2012
(millions)

Year	Inc. VAP	Inc. Reg. Voters	Inc. Turnout
2012*	8.4	na	-5.8
2008	9.8	4.2	5.4
2004	**13.1**	**12.6**	**14.9**
2000	9.0	1.8	5.8
1996	8.0	1.1	-8.8
1992	7.6	8.0	11.6
1988	8.1	2.5	0.3
1984	12.9	11.1	8.8
1980	10.5	7.3	6.4
1976	10.3	-.7	0.9
1972	19.7	11.9	6.8

Sources: US Census Bureau Current Population Survey, 2000-2008 Tables; *2012 extrapolated using 2010 to 2011 ACS 1 Yr. Data

Note: Values are rounded to the nearest single decimal point; na = not available

The first apparent observation is that the increases of 1972 to 1984 do not appear to translate into a substantial increase in turnout. The 1992 election does show a substantial increase in turnout. However, the increase in turnout in 1992 is not tied to an increase in voting age population or voter registration. The election of 1992 was a relatively unusual election where three major candidates vied for the presidency. Most likely, the 1992 increase was due to existing registered but *infrequent* voters turning out for the unique presidential race with three major candidates (i.e., Bush, Clinton, and Perot).

That being said, the significant increase from 2000 to 2004 is the only election year that shows a substantial increase in voting age population that seems to translate into a substantial increase in registered voters *and* a substantial increase in turnout. Other election years may have had a significant increase in voting age population *or* registered voters, but they did not translate into an increase in turnout. Alternatively, other election years may have had an increase in turnout but no substantial increase for both voting age population and registration. The election period of 2000 to 2004 is the only period that reflects a substantial increase for all three voting populations.

Viewing the changes in voting age population, registration, and turnout from 1972 to 2000 reminds one of how extraordinary the presidential trend is. Through all of the fluctuations in voting population, the popular vote for the Democratic candidate for president remains consistently linear. This reaffirms that this is truly a unique voting phenomenon.

To summarize, the extraordinary increase of voting age population in 2004 appears to translate to an extraordinary increase in voter registration *and* an extraordinary increase in voter turnout.

Since it is now determined that there exists a significant increase in turnout, there is one more component that should be analyzed. If there was an increase in voting age population that translated to an increase in turnout, it makes sense that there should also be an increase in *first-time* voters. In addition, with total first-time voters determined, the amount apportioned to the Democratic candidate also can be reviewed.

However, it is noticed that the increase in turnout in 2004 is higher than the increase in registered voters or even the increase in voting age population. Why? This could only mean that the increase in 2004 is due to more than the increase in voting age population or registration. Where do the additional voters come from? Some of the voters who turned out must have been existing registered but infrequent voters or voter who crossed over from the non-Democratic electorate.

The key to potentially solving the question of where these new Democratic voters came from may lie with the *first-time* voters. Thus, first-time voter analysis is performed next.

What Occurred with First-Time Voters?

Data for first-time voters are accessible only as far back as 1984. Nonetheless, national exit polls reveal that from 1984 to 2000 the percentage of first-time voters ranges from 6 to 9 percent (see Table 14-6). The average during that time period is 8 percent. However, in 2004 and 2008 the percentage of first-time voters increases to 11 percent.

Once again, the increase from 2000 to 2004 is the highest increase for the years that are analyzed. This coincides with the increase in voter age population. Since first-time voters are most likely new registered voters, the unusual increase in voting age population that translated to new registered voters ultimately produces an unusual number of first-time voters.

Table 14-6 US Pres. Election First-Time Voter Increase, 1984 to 2012 (millions)

Year	First-Time Voters (est.)	First-Time Voter, %	Inc. First-Time Voters (est.)
2012	10.8	9	-2.9
2008	13.9	11	0.7
2004	13.2	11	3.8
2000	9.4	9	0.8
1996	8.6	9	2.3
1992	6.3	6	0.0
1988	6.3	7	-1.1
1984	7.3	8	na

Sources: New York Times exit poll data; Reuters/Ipsos exit poll data; US Census Bureau Current Population Survey, 2000 to 2008 & Voting & Registration in the November 2008 Election Online Tables

Note: Values are rounded to the nearest single decimal point.

At this point, once again, it is noticed that the increase in first-time voters from 2000 to 2004 is only a portion of the increase in turnout. From 2000 to 2004, the total of first-time voters increased to 3.8 million. Exit of

2004 polls reveals that the Democratic candidate received 53 percent of the first-time voters. This amount equates to an increase of approximately 2 million voters of first-time voters while the turnout in 2004 for the Democratic candidate has an additional 5 million voters from the projected trend (see Table 14-1). Just as the increase in turnout indicates the increase, first-time Democratic voters did not fully cause the trend to deviate as much as it did in 2004. A portion of the increase comes from the increase in first-time voters, but the remaining portion must have come from *infrequent* or voters from the non-Democratic electorate. In order to determine the origin of these additional voters, some type of analysis of whether the electorate remained fractured is require.

Is the Electorate Still Fractured?

Reviewing Fig. 14-1 clearly shows that the presidential trend has ended. In addition, the previous section shows that there had been a step-level increase voting age population that partially translated into a step-level vote increase for the Democratic candidate (and most likely non-Democratic candidates as well). However, does this mean that the electorate was no longer fractured? Or is it simply that the voting population of the country increases for both electorates?

To verify whether the electorate remains fractured, the initial analysis used to verify the existence of the fracturing is applied. To review, the voting electorate for presidential elections had fractured into two parts. One part, the Democratic electorate, included mostly voters who only voted for the Democratic candidate. Because the popular vote for the Democratic candidate for president was essentially Democratic voters, each subsequent election was made up of mostly voters who voted for the Democratic candidate in the previous election plus the first-time Democratic voters for the current election. Only a smaller group of voters swung back and forth from the Democratic electorate and the second part, the non-Democratic electorate.

Figure 14-7 revisits the first-time voter analysis using data for the 1984 to 2000 elections. Using exit polls from 1984 to 2000 as well as the total popular vote, percentage of first-time voters, and partisan portion of those voters, the numbers of first-time voters for each party designation are estimated.

The projected amount for the Democratic popular vote is calculated by adding the popular vote of the Democratic candidate's previous election plus the exit polls of first-time voters for the projected election year. The same projection is determined for the Republican candidates as well. In addition, a percentage accuracy of the projected popular vote is derived. As Table 14-7 indicates, the accuracy of adding the number of first-time voters plus the previous popular vote for the Democratic candidates' projections for 1984 to 2000 is no less than 95.4 percent with an average of 97.5 percent. During the same period, the accuracy for the Republican candidates is as low as 69.9 percent with an average of 83.5 percent.

Applying the same techniques to the years of 2000 to 2008 yields accuracy for the Democratic candidates' projections from 97.4 to 98.5 percent with an average of 97.8 percent (see Table 14-8). The Republican candidates from 2000 to 2008 average 87.8 percent and vary from 85.8 to 91.1 percent.

Table 14-7 Estimate of First-Time Voters & Accuracy of Popular Vote Proj., 1984 to 2000

	1984	1988	1992	1996	2000
Total Vote (M)	92.7	91.6	104.4	96.3	105.4
First-Time Voter (Exit Polls, %)	8	7	6	9	9
First-Time Dem Voters (Exit Polls, %)	38	47	46	54	52
First-Time Rep Voters (Exit Polls, %)	61	51	32	34	43
First-Time Ind Voters (Exit Polls, %)	na	na	22	11	4
First-Time Dem Voters (est.)	2.8	3.0	2.9	4.7	4.9
First-Time Rep Voters (est.)	4.5	3.3	2.0	2.9	4.1
First-Time Ind Voters (est.)	na	na	1.4	1.0	0.4
Total Dem Voters Actual (M)	37.6	41.8	44.9	47.4	51.0
Total Dem Voters, est. proj. (M)	38.3	40.6	44.7	49.6	52.3
Accuracy% of Democratic proj.	**98.1**	**97.1**	**99.5**	**95.4**	**97.4**
Total Rep Voters Actual (M)	54.5	48.9	39.1	39.2	50.5
Total Rep Voters, proj. (M)	48.4	57.7	50.9	42.1	43.3
Accuracy, % of Republican, proj.	**88.9**	**81.9**	**69.9**	**92.7**	**85.8**

Sources: *New York Times* exit polls (1984 to 2000); US Census Bureau Statistical Abstract 2004; uselectionatlas.org

Note: na = values not available or too small

Just as the accuracies for the elections from 1972 to 2000, the Democratic candidates' projections continued to be higher than the accuracy of the Republican candidates. The averages of the accuracies for both the Democratic and Republican candidates' projections from 2000 to 2008 are higher than the average from 1972 to 2000 (97.8 and 87.9 percent, respectively).

Although there is an altering and a *bending* of the Democratic popular vote trend (as shown in Fig. 14-1), the projections using first-time voters validate that the fracturing of the electorate still existed until 2008.

Evidence that the fracturing of the electorate continued to exist is demonstrated by the Democratic popular vote continuing to be accurately projected by added the previous election plus the new first-time voters. It is simply that there is an extraordinary increase in voters, specifically from 2000 to 2004, which translates into a step-level increase in the Democratic and possibly the non-Democratic candidates' popular vote.

Table 14-8 Estimate of First-Time Voters & Accuracy of Popular Vote Proj., 2000 to 2012

	2000	2004	2008	2012
Total Vote	105.4	122.3	127.3	128.1
First-Time Voter (Exit Polls, %)	9	11	11	9
First-Time Dem Voters (Exit Polls, %)	52	53	69	66
First-Time Rep Voters (Exit Polls, %)	43	45	30	33
First-time Ind Voters (Exit Polls, %)	4	na	na	na
First-Time Dem Voters (est.)	4.9	7.1	9.7	7.2
First-Time Rep Voters (est.)	4.1	6.1	4.2	3.6
First-Time Ind Voters (est.)	0.4	na	na	na
Total Dem Voters Actual (M)	51.0	59.0	67.0	63.7
Total Dem Voters, est. proj. (M)	52.3	58.1	68.7	74.2
Accuracy% of Democratic, proj.	**97.4**	**98.5**	**97.5**	83.4
Total Rep Voters Actual (M)	50.5	62.0	58.5	59.8
Total Rep Voters, proj. (M)	43.3	56.5	66.2	62.1
Accuracy, % of Republican, proj.	**85.8**	**91.1**	**86.7**	**96.1**

Sources: New York Times exit polls (2000 to 2008); Reuters/Ipsos 2012 exit poll data; uselectionatlas.org (2012 election results as of December 10, 2012)

Note: na = values not available or too small; (M) = million

However, in 2012 the accuracy of the Democratic candidate's popular vote projections dramatically dropped to its lowest point since the trend began…a meager 83.4 percent. At the same time, the Republican projection was an impressive 96.1 percent. This begs the question: What happened to the Democratic popular vote in 2012?

What Occurred in 2012?

One of the biggest unresolved questions in this book is why was the popular vote for the Democratic candidate, Barack Obama, so low in 2012? To view the vote for the Democratic candidate graphically, review Fig. 14-3. The graph clearly shows the votes cast for the Democratic candidates steadily increasing in a linear fashion from 1972 to 2000. The popular vote then begins to bend upward from 2000 to 2008. However, after 2008 the vote decreases in 2012. This is truly an inconsistency.

The term "inconsistency" is intentionally used to put this decrease in popular vote into perspective. The popular vote in 2012 was the **first-time** that the Democratic candidate's popular vote decreased in 40 years, excluding the 1976 election. The 2012 popular vote decrease or drop-off is certainly not consistent with every other election since 1972.

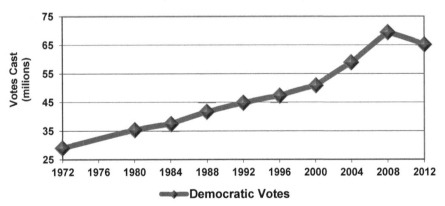

**Democratic Popular Vote
(1972 to 2012 w/o 1976)**

Sources: US Census Bureau Statistical Abstracts 2010 and uselectionatlas.org

Figure 14-3 Democratic Popular Vote
(1972 to 2012, w/o 1976)

Nevertheless, what caused this inconsistency to occur? Could there have been a reversal of what occurred in 2004? That is to say, instead of an extraordinary increase as in 2000 to 2004, did a significant *decrease* occur in voting age population occur? Could a certain group of voters have made a decision to significantly *not* vote for Barack Obama (see Figure 14-4)? Unfortunately, data are not available at this writing to fully determine the answer. All of these possibilities need to be investigated and resolved and will be covered in future publications.

Did the Demographic Trends Continue from 2000?

After 2000, did the same demographic trends as shown in Chap. 13 continue? Figure 14-4 reveals the answer. Overall, the trends remain the same. The Democratic candidate's minority vote continued to increase at a relatively rapid pace. The white vote for the Democratic candidate continued to increase until 2012 where it took a dip downward. Both the minority and the white votes cast for the non-Democratic candidate votes were fairly stable from 2000 to 2012 except for the slight increase in 2004. Thus, the popular vote patterns from 1972 to 2000 essentially continued to 2012.

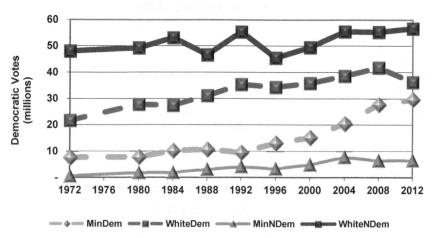

Sources: New York Times exit poll data (1980 to 2012); uselectionatlas.org

Figure 14-4 White & Minority Dem/Non-Dem Votes Cast.
(1972 to 2012, w/o 1976)

The next graphs to review are the breakdown trend lines by major race/ethnicity. Figures 14-5 and 14-6 for the trend lines from 1972 to 2012 show similar results as the trend lines for 1972 to 2000 contained in Figures. 13-14 and 13-15, respectively. Both sets of graphs show similar trends. The presidential trend lines indicate that each major race/ethnicity is trending *increasingly* for the Democratic candidates. Conversely, each non-Democratic candidates' trend lines are decreasing.

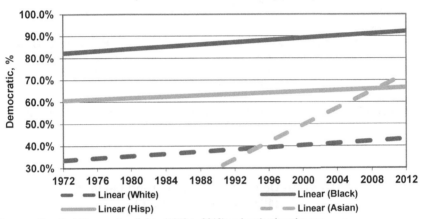

Sources: *New York Times* exit poll data (1972 to 2012) and uselectionatlas.org

Figure 14-5 Democratic Popular Vote Trend Lines by Race/Ethnicity, %
(1972 to 2012, w/o 1976)

The answer as to whether the demographic trends continue clearly is yes. The trend lines from 1972 to 2012 for *every major race/ethnicity group are moving in a increasing fashion for the Democratic candidates and decreasing for the non-Democratic candidates.* This leaves just one set of trend lines to create: the total popular vote percentage for the Democratic and non-Democratic candidates. If all major race/ethnicity groups indicate an increase for the Democratic candidates, so *should* the combined percentages. In fact, this is the case. Figure 14-7 displays the stark trend lines for the Democratic and non-Democratic candidates' percentage from 1972 to 2012. The Democratic candidates' trend lines exhibit the same pattern as those of the major individual race/ethnicity trends. The next chapter expands on the implication of this astonishing graph and the potential future of presidential elections.

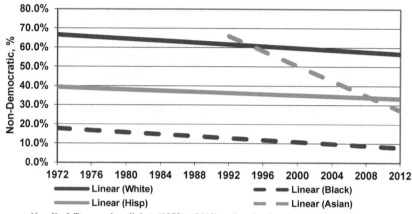

Sources: New York Times exit poll data (1972 to 2012) and uselectionatlas.org

Figure 14-6 Non-Democratic Popular Vote Trend Lines by Race/Ethnicity, %
(1972 to 2012, w/o 1976)

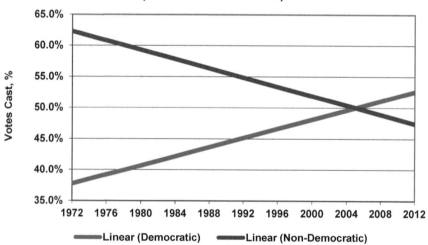

Sources: US Census Bureau Statistical Abstracts 2010 and uselectionatlas.org

Figure 14-7 Dem/Non-Dem Popular Vote Trend Lines, %
(1972 to 2012, w/o 1976)

Chapter 15

2016 and Future Implications

Introduction

Undoubtedly, a second and arguably more interesting question lingering in most peoples' minds after reading through the other chapters in this book may be what will be the outcome for the Democratic candidate in 2016 or beyond? Undeniably, the presidential trend of 1972 to 2000 ended in 2000. In addition, from 2000 to 2008 there may have been a start of a new trend. However, in 2012 this new trend ended. Thus, what is in store for 2016 or even after that election?

Analyzing Using Votes Cast Percentage

Projecting the Democratic *popular vote* for 2016 is questionable at this point. With the increase in 2000 to 2008 and then the decrease of 2012, the predictability of the popular vote has become unclear. However, could there be another method of projecting the voting outcome for the Democratic candidate?

Since the trend has ended, does any predictability remain? The short answer is yes. First, consider that the popular vote for the Democratic candidate was predictable up until the election of 2000. Up until that time, the popular vote for the Democratic candidate was predictable with a high accuracy (see Chap. 7). Therefore, half of the electorate was predictable until 2000.

Second, the electorate has remained fractured (see Chap. 14). This means that the bulk of the Democratic votes are isolated from the non-Democratic candidates and vice versa. The effect of the continued fracturing and the previous linear popular vote should reduce the fluctuation of the votes cast.

Figure 15-1 displays the Democratic and non-Democratic popular vote on the same graph. The graph shows the relative consistent increasing votes cast for the Democratic candidates while the non-Democratic candidates fluctuate. The consistent progression of the Democratic candidates' votes cast should bode well for the predictability of the electorate.

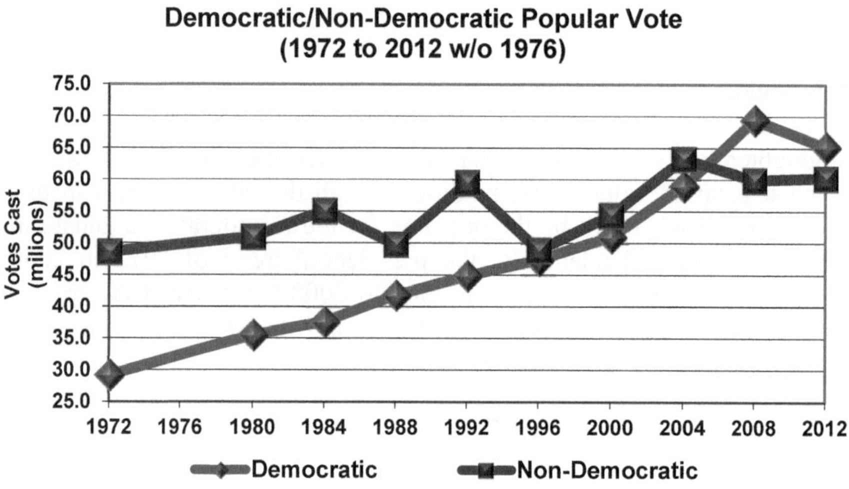

Democratic/Non-Democratic Popular Vote (1972 to 2012 w/o 1976)

Sources: US Census Bureau Statistical Abstracts 2010 and uselectionatlas.org

Figure 15-1 Democratic/Non-Democrat Popular Vote
(1972 to 2012, w/o 1976)

That being said, the Democratic popular vote may not be an accurate method of predicting the candidates' voting outcome. Nonetheless, Fig. 13-16 provides a clue to predicting candidates' votes cast even after the trend ended. The clue is to use the Democratic and non-Democratic candidates' *percentage* of votes cast instead of the popular vote amount.

Figure 15-2 shows the Democratic and non-Democratic percentage of votes cast from 1972 to 2012 (with 1976 removed). Although the popular vote percentage fluctuates from election year to election year, it is not substantial. The fluctuation of the votes cast percentage is minimized due to the continued fracturing of the electorate in addition to half of the electorate (Democratic side) increasing in a linear manner for most the time.

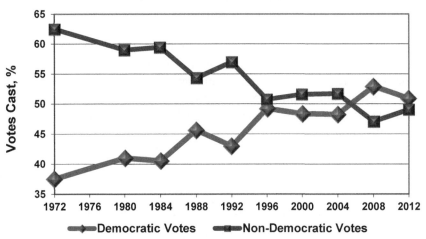

Sources: US Census Bureau Statistical Abstracts 2010 and uselectionatlas.org

Figure 15-2 Democratic/Non-Democratic Candidates' Votes Cast, %
(1972 to 2012, w/o 1976)

The graph clearly displays two steady 40-year upward and downward trends for the Democratic and non-Democratic candidates, respectively. Are these trend percentages consistent enough to provide election projections?

Projecting the 2012 Election's Votes Cast Percentage

Previously, the popular vote for the next election for the Democratic candidate is found to be predictable and follows a fairly linear trend line from 1972 to 2000 (see Chap. 7). What about votes cast percentage? Did the percentage of votes cast follow closely with its trend line? If the percentage of votes cast is linear, the trend line should be able to estimate the election percentage. In addition, if the trend line is extended, it should be able to project the next election. Although these projections are not as sophisticated as the prediction models that Nate Silver uses (creator of fivethirtyeight.com), they appear to be accurate nonetheless.

In order for votes cast percentages to accurately project the next election, the r^2 values for the trend line must be significantly high. Once calculated, the r^2value of the Democratic and non-Democratic popular vote percentages from 1972 to 2008 turn out to be a very respectable 0.8890. Thus, the trend line (linear regression) equations for 1972 to 2008 should be able to provide adequate projections for 2012.

Using the equation derived from the trend line from 1972 to 2008 and calculating the estimated popular vote for the Democratic candidate, the estimated votes cast is accurate within range of -2.34% to 2.28%. Table 15.1 presents the estimated Democratic candidate's percentage along with the *absolute* error percentage and hi/lo range estimates for each election year.

Table 15-1 Estimated Democratic Popular Vote Percentage & Hi/Lo Percentage Projections, 1972 to 2008

	1972	1980	1984	1988	1992	1996	2000	2004	2008
Actual Dem, %	37.5	41.0	40.6	45.6	43.0	49.2	48.4	48.3	52.9
Est. Dem, %	37.3	40.5	42.1	43.8	45.4	47.0	48.6	50.2	51.8
Dem Diff, %	0.18	0.46	-1.59	1.90	-2.34	2.28	-0.17	-1.88	1.17
Est. Dem, % Hi	39.7	42.9	44.5	46.1	47.7	49.3	50.9	52.5	54.1
Est. Dem, % Lo	35.1	38.3	39.9	41.5	43.1	44.7	46.3	47.9	49.5

Sources: US Census Bureau Statistical Abstracts 2010 and uselectionatlas.org

Note: Although table shows one or two decimal places, calculations are determined using multiple decimal places.

Using the trend line from 1972 to 2008, the projected popular vote percentage for the Democratic candidate, Barack Obama, in 2012 is calculated. The result is 53.35 percent (see Table 15-2).

Table 15-2 Projected Democratic Popular Vote Percentage in 2012 Using 1972 to 2008 Trend Line

	2012 Estimates (1972 to 2008) Trend, %
Democratic Projection for 2012	**53.35**
Dem High Proj. (+2.28%)	55.64
Dem Low Proj. (-2.34%)	51.01
Dem Actual %	51.01

Sources: US Census Bureau Statistical Abstracts 2010 and uselectionatlas.org

The high-end of the error percentage from 1972 to 2008 is 2.28, while the low-end error percentage is -2.34. This places the high projected amount at 55.64 percent and the low projected amount at 51.01 percent. The actual percentage that Barack Obama obtained is 51.01 percent.

The projected popular vote percentage for Obama for 2012 falls right on the low end of the projected value. The fact that the projected amount falls on the low projected value brings additional attention to the amount of votes cast that decreased from 2008 to 2012. However, the projected amount sufficiently estimates the popular vote for the Democratic candidate within the error range of the 1972 to 2008 trend. Next, how would projecting the 2016 popular vote percentage fare?

Projecting the 2016 Election's Popular Vote Percentage

In order to project the popular vote percentages for the 2016 election, the trend line needed to be extended from 1972 to 2012. The r^2 for the 1972 to 2012 trend line is only slightly lower than the trend line from 1972 to 2008 with a value of 0.8878. The r^2 value continues to reflect a relatively linear trend.

The 1972 to 2012 trend line is slightly different from the one from 1972 to 2008. Nonetheless, just as the trend line from 1972 to 2008 projected every popular vote percentage for the Democratic candidate within a relatively low error percentage, the 1972 to 2012 trend line did the same (see Table 15-3).

Table 15-3 Estimated Democratic Popular Vote Percentage & Hi/Lo Percentage Projections, 1972 to 2012

	1972	1980	1984	1988	1992	1996	2000	2004	2008	2012
Act. Dem, %	37.5	41.0	40.6	45.6	43.0	49.2	48.4	48.3	52.9	51.0
Est. Dem, %	37.7	40.7	42.2	43.7	45.2	46.6	48.1	49.6	51.1	52.6
Dem Diff, %	-0.22	0.30	-1.64	1.97	-2.16	2.59	0.25	-1.35	1.83	-1.57
Est. Dem, % Hi	40.3	43.3	44.8	46.3	47.7	49.2	50.7	52.2	53.7	55.2
Est. Dem, % Lo	35.6	38.6	40.0	41.5	43.0	44.5	46.0	47.5	48.9	50.4

Sources: US Census Bureau Statistical Abstracts 2010 and uselectionatlas.org

Note: Although table shows one or two decimal places, calculations are determined using multiple decimal places

The popular vote percentage for the Democratic candidates for each election from 1972 to 2012 fell within the high and low range of the trend line. Will 2016 follow suite?

Extending the trend line to predict the popular vote for the 2016 popular vote percentage for the Democratic candidate yields a value of 54.07 percentage. However, the high- and low-end error percentage from 1972 to 2012 is -2.16 and +2.59 percent, respectively. When the error range is incorporated, the percentage of the popular vote for the Democratic candidate in 2016 should range between 56.65 and 51.91 percent.

Table 15-4 Projected Democratic Popular Vote Percentage for 2016 Using 1972 to 2012 Trend Line	
	2016 Estimates (1972 to 2012) Trend, %
Democratic Popular Vote % Projection for 2016	**54.07**
Dem High Proj. (+2.59%)	56.65
Dem Low Proj. (-2.16%)	51.91
Dem Actual%	???????

Sources: US Census Bureau Statistical Abstracts 2010 and uselectionatlas.org

As with the demographic trend lines shown in Chap. 13, the projections for the popular vote percentage for the Democratic candidates appear to be favorable for the Democratic candidate. Given these projections, the Democratic candidate should win the popular vote percentage in the 2016 election. This leaves one final question. Will the Democratic candidate also win the Electoral College votes?

The Presidential Trend and Major Battleground States

It is clear that the Democratic candidates stand a great chance in winning the popular vote for the 2016 election as well as future ones. However, what about winning the Electoral College? The key to winning the presidency lies with winning the majority of Electoral College votes. Winning the Electoral College votes over the last several election cycles has come down to winning the battleground states or *purple* states. Battleground states being those states where each candidate has a fair chance of winning the state. Purple states are typically defined as those states whose previous margin of victory is less than 6 percentage points.[104]

There are three recent battleground or purple states that remarkably display similarities with the national trend: Florida, Ohio, and Virginia (see Fig. 15-3). In 2012, these states represented a combined total of 60 electoral votes. A review of the three states' respective r^2 values for the Democratic popular vote from 1972 to 2000 yields a fairly close match with the nation's. Florida is .9639, Ohio is .9893, and Virginia is .9785. The national r^2 value is .9970. Therefore, the r^2 values validate that the trend is clearly present in each of the three states and thus should make them excellent candidates to us in projecting the outcome.

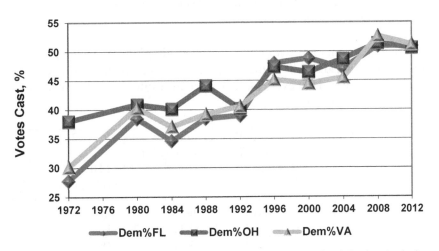

FL, OH & VA Democratic Popular Vote, %
(1972 to 2012 w/o 1976)

Sources: US Census Bureau Current Population Surveys; 2000-2008 & Voting & Registration in the November Election, uselectionatlas.org

Figure 15-3 Florida, Ohio and Virginia Democratic Popular Vote, % (1972 to 2012, w/o 1976)

---

[104] Alec M. Gallup, Frank Newport, *Gallup Poll, Public Opinion 2008*, Rowman & Littlefield Publishers, Inc., pg. 244

Since these three battleground states display a close match with the national r^2 values and thus depict a linear popular vote line, the hypothesis is that the percent for the Democratic candidates should also be similar. This turns out to be the case (see Fig. 15-3).

Figure 15-3 displays the percentage of the Democratic candidates' popular vote for the three states. Just as the national popular vote percentage performed, the states' percentages also trended in a similar manner from 1972 to 2012. Moreover, just as with the national trend, each percent line diverges to 50 percent or slightly above.

If the trend lines from 1972 to 2008 for the three states are used to predict the 2012 election, what would be the results? Table 15-5 shows the estimated projections as well as the high and low values for each major battleground state. As before, the high and low values are calculated using the minimum and maximum error percentage over the 1972 to 2008 election period.

The actual results are within the projected high/low range for each state except for Florida. All of the actual results are on the low end of the projected values. However, Florida's actual results are 1.3 percent lower than the low projection for the state.

Table 15-5 Projected Popular Vote Percentage in 2012
Using 1972 to 2008 Trend Line

	2012 Lo Projected (1972 to 2008) Trend, %	2012 Projected (1972 to 2008) Trend, %	2012 Hi Projected (1972 to 2008) Trend, %	2012 Actual Results, %
FL Dem Proj.	51.3	54.1	58.2	49.9
OH Dem Proj.	47.3	51.5	53.1	50.6
VA Dem Proj.	49.5	51.9	56.3	51.2

Sources: US Census Bureau Current Population Survey, 2000-2008 & Voting & Registration in the November Election, uselectionatlas.org

Be that as it may, the projections reveal that the Democratic candidate, Barack Obama, should have won each of these battleground states except for possibly Ohio. Barack Obama was projected to win Virginia in 2012 even though the low projections indicated a percentage under 50 percent

(49.5%) because at least 1 percent of the vote would be attributed to the Independent candidate. This would leave only 49.0 percent left for the Republican candidate. The low projection for Ohio may lead one to believe that Barack Obama could have lost the state. However, if Barack Obama won the battleground states of Florida and Virginia and lost Ohio, he would have still won reelection in 2012.

Turning to the next election, if the three states' trend lines are extended to include the 2012 election, the outcome percentage for the 2016 election for the Democratic candidates could be projected. Table 15-6 indicates that once again Ohio is the only state that the Democratic candidate should lose out of the three.

Table 15-6 Projected Democratic Popular Vote Percentage in 2016 Using 1972 to 2012 Trend Line			
	2016 Lo Projected (1972 to 2012) Trend, %	2016 Projected (1972 to 2012) Trend, %	2016 Hi Projected (1972 to 2012) Trend, %
FL Dem Proj.	49.9	55.0	57.0
OH Dem Proj.	47.1	52.6	52.9
VA Dem Proj.	49.4	53.6	56.0

Sources: US Census Bureau Current Population Survey, 2000-2008 & Voting & Registration in the November Election, uselectionatlas.org;

Although the projections indicate that all three states should be won by the Democratic candidate in 2016, Florida and Virginia seem to be the most likely to be won by the Democratic candidate. Furthermore, once again, if Ohio is not won by the Democratic candidate, but all other states are held on to, the Democratic candidate would win the electoral votes count and thus once again the presidency.

Final Thoughts on the Future Electorate

After all has been said and done, the prior projections are based upon percentages of those voters who *turn out* to vote. The projections do not include those voters who *did not turnout*. These trend lines *could* possibly alter *if* nonvoters are motivated to turn out. Also, certain voter groups (i.e. young and minority voters) may need the continuation of focused voter registration and get out the vote (GOTV) efforts in order for them to continue to turn out at the same rates.

In addition to the possibility of decreased voter registration and GOTV efforts, there exists a potential effect of new voter laws that have been enacted and continue to be enacted over the last two presidential elections. These laws potentially could modify the voting electorate by trimming or reducing the size of the electorate. This trimming could effect the Democratic electorate significantly more than the non-Democratic electorate. Specifically, studies have shown that the new laws could have the effect of disproportionately reducing poor and minority voters,[105] which undoubtedly would disproportionately decrease Democratic votes.

However, a politically somewhat cynical view of these new voter laws may be that this is the only comprehensive way to change the pending destiny of the outcome of presidential elections, albeit temporarily. It will be temporary because if the Democratic and non-Democratic voting electorates continue to follow the percentage trend lines, eventually, neither Republican nor Independent candidates will be capable of garnering enough votes to win the popular vote. At that time, in theoretical terms, the Democratic *voting* electorate will ultimately become larger than the non-Democratic Electorate. Reviewing again the graph in Fig. 15-2 substantiates the point. The trends for 40 years of the Democratic votes cast and their associated percentages have consistently moved toward overtaking the non-Democratic voting electorate.

In addition, Fig 15-2 may reveal another modern day political occurrence at the national level. Reviewing the graph, one could have predicted many years prior, what would occur when the Democratic votes cast and the non-Democratic votes cast (for the most part Republican) become very close or equal to each other in voter strength? The prediction would be that major conflict and strife would occur at the national or specifically, federal political level (i.e. presidential & congress). Could this graph explain why it seems as though a segment of congress and the president have moved to a high level of unpleasant political discourse?

---

[105] Wendy R. Weiser and Lawrence Norden, *Voting Law Changes in 2012*, Brennan Center for Justice, 2011

In essence, to paraphrase what Sun Tzu said in the *Art of War* over two thousand years ago, *"If equally matched, do battle… "*[106] Hence, applying Sun Tzu's philosophy to the field of politics, the current voting configuration is primed for conflict at the national level. Reviewing the graph contained in Fig 15-2 indicates that, at the national level, we are now in a point in time when the Democratic and non-Democratic voting electorates are almost equal in size and evenly *matched*.

Nonetheless, barring a *major* realignment shift in the electorate or major shift in *party policy*, the Democratic popular vote and percentages *have* or are about to consistently surpass the non-Democratic votes cast and percentage. After that point, the Democratic candidates for president should win and continue to win the popular vote until another significant political *realignment* of the electorate.[107]

In addition, the trend lines for the three major battleground states— Florida, Ohio, and Virginia—have progressed similarly to the national trends. If these trends continue, as shown in Fig. 15-3, the Democratic candidate should also win the electoral vote contest as well. In other words, if our electorate remains fractured, future Democratic candidates should enjoy popular vote success, electoral vote success, and the US presidency for many years to come.

---

[106] Sun Tzu translated by Thomas Cleary, *The Art of War*, Shambhula Publications, 1988

[107] There is a side-note to consider. It could very well be that the trend lines for the office of president could be the proverbial *canary in the coal mine*. In other words, the pending outcome of the trends for the Democratic and non-Democratic candidates will most likely manifest itself in the Senate and ultimately even in the House of Representatives.

2016 and Future Implications

APPENDICES

Appendix A:
National Presidential Election Results
(1948 to 2012, w/o 1976)
in millions

Table A-1 Presidential Election Results (1948, 1952, 1956, 1956, 1960)				
Year	1948	1952	1956	1960
Dem.	24.179347	27.375090	26.028028	34.220984
Rep.	21.991292	34.075529	35.579180	34.108157
Other	2.622896	0.301323	0.414120	0.503341
Total	48.793535	61.751942	62.021328	68.832482

Source: Leip, David *David Leip's Atlas of US Presidential Election*, www.uselectionatlas.org

Table A-2 Presidential Election Results (1964, 1968, 1972, 1980)				
Year	1964	1968	1972	1980
Dem.	43.127041	31.271839	29.173222	35.480115
Rep.	27.175754	31.783783	47.168710	43.903230
Other	0.336489	10.144376	1.402095	7.126333
Total	70.639284	73.199998	77.744027	86.509678

Source: Leip, David *David Leip's Atlas of US Presidential Elections*, www.uselectionatlas.org

Table A-3 Presidential Election Results (1984, 1988, 1992, 1996)				
Year	1984	1988	1992	1996
Dem.	37.577352	41.809476	44.909806	47.400125
Rep.	54.455472	48.886597	39.104550	39.198755
Other	0.620409	0.898613	20.409567	9.676521
Total	92.653233	91.594686	104.423923	96.275401

Source: Leip, David *David Leip's Atlas of US Presidential Elections*, www.uselectionatlas.org

Appendices A: Presidential Election Results

Table A-4 Presidential Election Results (2000, 2004, 2008, 2012)				
Year	2000	2004	2008	2012
Dem.	51.003926	59.028439	69.058185	65.917257
Rep.	50.460110	62.040610	59.700776	60.932235
Other	3.953439	1.224499	1.931440	2.365929
Total	105.417475	122.293548	130.690401	129.215421

Source: Leip, David *David Leip's Atlas of US Presidential Elections,* www.uselectionatlas.org

References

Apple, R.W., Jr., *New York Times*. (2004). http://www.nytimes.com/2004/08/30/politics/campaign/30apple.html

Breipohl, Arthur M. (1970). *Probabilistic Systems Analysis*, John Wiley & Sons, New York.

Business Week (1951). *Business Week*.

Campbell, Angus. (1960). *The American Voter*, University of Chicago Press

Sun Tzu translated by Cleary, Thomas (1988). *The Art of War*, Shambhula Publications

Fair, Ray C. (2002). *Predicting Presidential Elections and Other Things*, Stanford University Press

Gardener, Michael. (2002). *Harry Truman and Civil Rights*, Southern Illinois University Press

Greenhaven Press's Ten Book series. (2004). *The Turbulent 60s*

Gravetter, Frederick J. & Wallnau, Larry B. (1996). *Statistics for the Behavior Sciences, West Publishing*, Fourth Edition, St. Paul, MN

Leip, David. (2004). *David Leip's Atlas of US Presidential Elections*, http://www.uselectionatlas.org

Library of Congress, *African American Odyssey: The Civil Rights Era* (2004). http://memory.loc.gov/ammem/aaohtml/exhibit/aopart9.html. Washington, D.C.

Meyers, William P. (2004). *A Brief History of the Democratic Party*.

Moncur, Michael. (2005). *Michael Moncur's (Cynical) Quotations*, http://www.quotationspage.com

References

Microsoft Corporation. (2005). *Vietnam War, Microsoft® Encarta® Online Encyclopedia 2005.* http://encarta.msn.com © 1997-2005

The New York Times, Edison Media Research Mitofsky International, http://elections.nytimes.com/2008/results/president/exit-polls.html

Price, Geoff. (2004). *Assessing the Vote and the Roots of American Political Divide.* http://www.rationalrevolution.net/articles/assessing_the_vote_and_the_r oots.htm

The National Election Studies, Center for Political Studies, University of Michigan. (2000). *The NES Guide to Public Opinion and Electoral Behavior.* http://www.umich.edu/~nes/nesguide/nesguide.htm. Ann Arbor, MI: University of Michigan, Center for Political Studies [producer and distributor]

US Census Bureau. (2001). *Current Population Survey*

US Census Bureau. (2002). *Demographic Trends in the 20th Century*

US Census Bureau. (2004-2005). *Statistical Abstract of the United States* (Table No. HS-52)

US Census Bureau. (2004-2010). *Voting & Registration in the November 2004 Election* Online Tables

Index

Index

CPSIA information can be obtained at www.ICGtesting.com
Printed in the USA
LVOW01s1724141113

361206LV00001B/1/P